T0131663

AWAKE CHRISTIANS!

CELESTE PEREZ

WESTBOW
PRESS®
A DIVISION OF THOMAS NELSON
& ZONDERVAN

WestBow Press books may be ordered through booksellers or by contacting:

WestBow Press
A Division of Thomas Nelson & Zondervan
1663 Liberty Drive
Bloomington, IN 47403
www.westbowpress.com
844-714-3454

ISBN: 978-1-6642-5729-0 (sc)
ISBN: 978-1-6642-5730-6 (hc)
ISBN: 978-1-6642-5728-3 (e)

Library of Congress Control Number: 2022902602

Print information available on the last page.

WestBow Press rev. date: 03/21/2022

In honor of my deceased mother, Gladys, who gave us her unconditional motherly love, dedication, patience, and angelic being.

CONTENTS

Introduction ix

Chapter 1 The Fulfillment of the Seed................................. 1
Chapter 2 The Power of Jesus 13
Chapter 3 The Resurrection of Jesus................................... 19
Chapter 4 The Birth of Christianity.................................... 33
Chapter 5 Where is the Power of the Church? 39
Chapter 6 A Common Evil among Christians 51
Chapter 7 Awake.. 57
Chapter 8 Arise.. 65
Chapter 9 Shine 73
Chapter 10 Defending Christianity 81

Conclusion.. 93
Bibliography 95

INTRODUCTION

As Christians, we live in critical times where we need to be firm in Christ Jesus more than ever. The purpose of this book is to inspire Christians around the world not to lose track of who they are in Christ, pursue with fire the will of God in their lives, and fulfill their ministry. God fulfilled His promises concerning the Son of Man, which took a trajectory of centuries, but it proves to us that He is a God of promises, and His words do not return void.

Jesus fulfilled His ministry and gave us an example to follow. Even more, just like God used the prophets to announce the coming of the Messiah, Jesus commanded His disciples to wait for the promise, and as we know, the promise came to pass. Jesus told His disciples that a Second Coming would occur. In their writings, the apostles assured that an event such as the Second Coming of Christ is inevitable. The church that God will raise will be ready for the Second Coming. But, is today's church that church? Absolutely not!

Many Christians in today's church are spiritually tired, fatigued, or sleeping. Many Christians have lost their first love, their fire for Jesus and are consumed with worries of the world. God has given the church power, and my concern is why the church is not using the power. What is preventing Christians from experiencing God's power in their lives? What is preventing

Christians from demonstrating to others the power of God so others may know God?

This book will illustrate how the early church (also referred to as the primitive church) took advantage of the scripture, took advantage of the power, and fulfilled their ministry. Even through persecutions, the primitive church prevailed in their Christian beliefs. We have the power through Jesus Christ. His resurrection still testifies that He is alive and ready to help Christians worldwide conquer their fears and advance the kingdom.

Evil is in the atmosphere, but true Christians stand against it. We are to be Christians who give good testimony that advances the gospel, not evildoers. Therefore, I encourage Christians around the world to awake, rise, shine, and defend Christ.

CHAPTER ONE

THE FULFILLMENT OF THE SEED

And I will put enmity between you and the woman, and between your seed and her Seed; he shall bruise your head, and you shall bruise his heel.
—GENESIS 3:15[1]

Today, there are billions of people who profess to be Christian. Christianity has its history, and to understand Christianity, you have to understand its origins. God created the universe and everything in it. God also created Lucifer, a splendid creature who brought light to the glory of God. Lucifer was once known as the son of the morning. His pride and desire to take the place of God caused God to throw him out of heaven along with one-third of the angels. Lucifer, now is Satan, ruler of the darkness. The one-third of the angels which were kicked out with Lucifer became fallen angels, principalities, powers, rulers of darkness, spiritual hosts, or demons.

God created Adam and Eve for fellowship with Him and gave

---

[1] Unless otherwise noted, all biblical passages referenced are in the New King James Version (Nashville: HarperCollins Christian Publishing, 1982).

them rulership over all the kingdoms of the earth. Adam and Eve's disobedience to God's instructions resulted in mankind's fall from God's grace. As a result of mankind's fall, God cursed the serpent.

After the fall, God confronted Adam, Eve, and the serpent. Each of them received a sentence for their actions. God told the serpent that there would be enmity between the seed of the woman and his seed. As a result, Adam would experience hardship while working the land. And Eve would experience difficulty giving birth.

In Genesis 3:15, God declared these powerful words, "And I will put enmity between you and the woman, and between your seed and her Seed; he shall bruise your head, and you shall bruise His heel." These words would prepare the way for His Word (Jesus), would become flesh. Thus, "There is good New Testament authority for seeing here the protevangelium, the first glimmer of the gospel."[2]

Even more, "the New Testament will unmask the figure of Satan behind the serpent (Romans 16:20; Revelation 12:9; 20:2) and show the significance of the passing over of Adam for the woman and her seed (Matthew 1:23; Galatians 4:4; and 1 Timothy 2:15)."[3]

God, in His mercy and love, did not allow the serpent to think he had damaged everything good God created; instead, God demonstrated that new things were taking place. I love when God tells Isaiah, "Behold, the former things have come to pass, and new things I declare; before they spring forth I tell you of them" (Isaiah 42:9). God gave the sentence, but the fall did not stop God from demonstrating that He is loving and merciful. The fall of man did not hinder God from declaring new things because He is a good God.

[2] Derek Kidner, *Genesis: An Introduction and Commentary* (Downers Grove, IL: IVP Academic, 1967), 75.
[3] Kidner, 75.

As time passed, God saw that the hearts of humans were inclined to evil. Yet God was determined to keep His plan to make peace with humans. In the background, the genealogy of Jesus was in full motion. From Adam to the Second Adam, God was already working His divine plan to offer salvation to humanity. That is why God revealed Himself to Abram, whose name was later changed to Abraham.

When all the nations of the earth were pagan, God made a nation that would only serve Him. Abraham, known as the father of faith, changed the history of his life, his descendants, and his adoptive children of faith by his obedience. Because of his faith, Abraham is the father of our faith (Romans 4:16).

From Abraham to Joseph, a nation was born known as the Hebrews; they were in bondage in Egypt until God raised Moses to free them from slavery. The word *Hebrew* is found first in Genesis 14:13:

> Then one who had escaped came and told Abram the Hebrew, for he dwelt by the terebinth trees of Mamre the Amorite, brother of Eshcol and brother of Aner; and they were allies with Abram.

Hebrew means "I am a foreigner or a wanderer."

When God called Abraham, God pulled Abraham from his known territory to wander to an unknown territory that had been given to him by faith. God told Abraham that his descendants would be strangers in a land that was not theirs. Instead, they would serve the Egyptians, who would afflict them for four hundred years.

Abraham's grandson, Jacob, acknowledged that he dwelled in the land of Hebrews as a stranger, as his father Isaac dwelled in Canaan's land (Genesis 37:1). Even Joseph, Jacob's son, understood the concept that he was a foreigner in Egypt. Joseph knew that his origin was in the land of the Hebrews.

Jacob replied to Pharaoh,

> The days of the years of my pilgrimage are one hundred and thirty years; few and evil have been the days of the years of my life, and they have not attained to the days of the years of the life of my fathers in the days of their pilgrimage. (Genesis 47:9)

The truth is that we are pilgrims here on earth. Primitive Christians grasped the kingdom's mindset and looked to God because they understood that we are here temporarily, yet looking forward to the spiritual things. 2 Corinthians 4:18 says, "while we do not look at the things which are seen, but at the things which are not seen. For the things which are seen are temporary, but the things which are not seen are eternal."

The leader God chose to deliver the Hebrews from their Egyptian bondage was Moses. God used Moses in mighty ways, and as a leader, he succeeded because God was with him. The Bible refers to Moses as a very humble man. Numbers 12:3 says, "Now the man Moses was very humble, more than all men who were on the face of the earth."

Unfortunately, Moses's disobedience kept him from entering the Promised Land; Joshua and Caleb were the only ones from that generation who could enter the Promised Land. After Moses's death, Joshua helped the Israelites (Hebrews) take possession of the land that God promised them. As the years passed, people died, new generations came in, old generations died, but God remained the same. The Israelites encountered many adversities and challenges. Enemies came from outside and within, rising against this nation, but God always reminded them that He was with them. God was determined to fulfill his divine purpose with this nation and with humanity.

After Joshua's death, the people of Israel turned their backs on God and followed other gods. God then raised judges to rule the nation of Israel. It was not very effective. The Israelites repeatedly turned away from God, and God repeatedly raised different judges to free them from the hands of their enemies.

God raised many prophets who voiced God's words, hoping that the people would always do His will. When the prophet and judge Samuel came into the picture, the people of Israel wanted to be like other nations and have a king. The people of Israel did not understand that they were different from other nations. God set them apart intentionally to be His chosen people, unique and different. However, the Israelites thought they were less than the other nations because they did not have a king, not knowing that the King of kings was their king.

They asked for a king, and God provided them with a king. His name was Saul, which means "asked for." After King Saul failed, God raised David, a man after God's own heart. King David foresaw the coming of the Messiah:

> The Lord said to my Lord, "Sit at my right hand, till I make your enemies your footstool." (Psalm 110:1)

Who is this Lord? The one and only Christ who changed the history of the world! David's throne became established, and his sons reigned. Israel became divided into two kingdoms; the north was the kingdom of Israel, and the south was the kingdom of Judah. Eventually, both kingdoms fell, but before their fall, God raised many prophets to warn them and prophesy about the Messiah's coming.

One of those prophets was Isaiah. He was right on with this prophecy:

Therefore the Lord Himself will give you a sign:
Behold, the virgin shall conceive and bear a Son
and shall call his name Immanuel. (Isaiah 7:14)

How was this possible? How could a virgin give birth? Humanity had never heard or seen such a thing, but God revealed His mighty power to humanity many times.

After his ordeal, Job could only answer God by saying, "I know that You can do everything and that no purpose of Yours can be withheld from you" (Job 42:2).

Jeremiah, known as the weeping prophet, said, "Ah, Lord God! Behold, You have made the heavens and the earth by Your great power and outstretched arm. There is nothing too hard for you" (Jeremiah 32:17).

God wanted the Israelites to understand that He is the only powerful God who created all things for His glory. So, saying that a virgin will conceive meant a supernatural event would take place.

The north and south kingdoms suffered greatly and went into captivity. The Assyrians took captive the kingdom of Israel, and the Babylonians took captive the kingdom of Judah. Once again, the people of Israel experienced captivity.

Their sin led them into captivity. God sent prophets to both kingdoms to see if they would repent, but the consequences of sin were evident as time passed. Men like Daniel and his friends remained loyal to God despite their captivity in a pagan nation. On one occasion, while in captivity to the Persian and Medes kingdoms, God raised Queen Esther and Mordecai to save the Israelites (also known as the Jews). Also, God raised men like Nehemiah, Ezra, and Zerubbabel to restore Jerusalem from ruins.

After the restoration of Jerusalem, the country was not the same. Different kingdoms replaced each other for a while. These were times of uncertainty. Jerusalem was exposed to many foreigners who were interested in their land and who made the people pay tributes or taxes. The Hebrew forefathers were wanderers or foreigners by faith. Now, other foreigners were trying to rule them by force.

The Intertestamental Period included four hundred years of silence, but God's plan and purpose was still in full force. We see this in the genealogy of Jesus, which Matthew provided from the side of Joseph. And Luke gave the genealogy of Jesus from the side of Mary. Politically, Israel was not established as it had been in the past. The Books of the Maccabees illustrate the situation that Israel faced in those days. The Roman Empire came into Jerusalem and took over the land. Still, some people were hopeful about the coming of the Messiah.

Spiritually, the country was divided. Subgroups such as the Pharisees, Sadducees, Essenes, and the Zealots were present in the first century. There are many references in the New Testament about these subgroups, such as the Pharisees, Sadducees, or the Zealots. The historian Josephus gives a detailed description of the Essenes, their beliefs, and their practices. Even though they believed in the God of their fathers and accepted Moses's law, many leaders were not exemplary figures to follow. Man-made rules were added to Moses's law as well, which only added burdens to the people of Israel. Socially, the country was not stable. Economically, the country was giving its best to the Romans, and in turn the native poor received crumbs from their land. God sent John the Baptist to prepare the way. He preached about repentance in a bold, loud, and clear way. After hearing his powerful preaching, people from the Jordan River regions came to repent, confessing their sins and accepting the baptism of water.

Even the birth of John the Baptist was a miracle from God. His mother was barren, and his parents were both well advanced in years. Additionally, the birth of Jesus was a miraculous event that came directly from God. How did this happen? Even Mary questioned it since she was a virgin.

The fulfillment of the seed spoken by God to Adam, Eve, and

the serpent in the early days of humanity had come to fruition. It is revealed when Gabriel appears to Mary

> The Holy Spirit will come upon you, and the power of the Highest will overshadow you; therefore, also, that Holy One who is to be born will be called the Son of God. (Luke 1:35)

The angel Gabriel is the same angel who brought good news to the parents of John the Baptist. This angel stood in the presence of God, and God directed Gabriel to give Mary the news. An angel of the Lord appeared to Joseph as well regarding the birth of Jesus.

The Son of God, Jesus the Messiah, came to earth and changed the course of humanity. The prophet Isaiah said, "I heard the voice of the Lord, saying: Whom shall I send, and who will go for Us? Then I said, 'Here am I! Send me" (Isaiah 6:8).

In heaven, God asked the same question, and the Son of God did not hesitate. Before, the people of Israel practiced the sacrifice of animals for their atonement. The practice of sacrificing animals became a joke over and over and was not taken seriously. Even the leaders were at fault, including the Pharisees, Sadducees, and scribes. Jesus called them hypocrites because they were evildoers, their hearts were far from God, and they sought men's glory.

The word *fulfillment* means the act or state of fulfilling. It also implies completion, realization, or consummation. The New King James Version uses it six times (Psalm 66:12, Ezekiel 12:23, Daniel 11:14, Daniel 12:6, Luke 1:45, and Romans 13:10). The word *fulfilled* is used seventy-five times and *fulfill* is used thirty-four times. The verb *fulfill* is used in three senses that merit special attention: an ethical sense of observing or meeting requirements; a prophetic sense of corresponding to what was promised, predicted, or foreshadowed; and a temporal sense related to the arrival of times ordained by God.[4] The focus in this book regarding the word fulfilled is that it is as something that God promised, predicted, and foreshadowed.

Why did God bother to demonstrate to humanity that He is a God who fulfills His promises? He did so because He loves us. A great example of this kind of love is parental love. Good parents will try to keep their word so their children will trust them. When God said, "And I will put enmity between you and the woman, and between your seed and her Seed; He shall bruise your head, and you shall bruise His heel" (Genesis 3:15), God was making a promise to humanity. God foreshadowed the things that would come for humanity.

Once God released these words, the enemy did not stand still. The devil came with a plan. One of his plans was to destroy the seed of the woman and to replace it with his seed. We see this example in Genesis 6:2-4, how "the sons of God saw the daughters of men that they were beautiful, and they took wives for themselves of all whom they chose." Some scholars believe that the reference of the Sons of God is to the fallen angels. The union of the fallen angels and the daughters of men produce giants. The word giants in Hebrew is Nephilim or N'filim (נְפִיל). Other scholars believe that the Sons of God refer to Seth's descendants, who took wives from Cain's descendants.

The word in Hebrew for seed is זֶרַע zera`, which means "seed," "sowing," "offspring," "descendants," "children," or "posterity." Throughout history, Satan has tried to raise his seed for evil purposes, but none of the attempts could impede the Messiah's coming.

Many were hoping to see the Messiah, including Simeon: "And it had been revealed to him by the Holy Spirit that he would not see death before he had seen the Lord's Christ" (Luke

---

[4] Charles Brand, Charles Draper, and Archie England, *Holman Illustrated Bible Dictionary* (Nashville: Holman Bible Publishers, 2003), s.v. "fulfill."

2:26). Luke mentions a woman named Anna; she was eighty-four years old, widowed, and a prophetess. She dedicated her life to serving in the temple. Even more, she prayed and fasted day and night. What a testimony! When she saw Jesus, she spoke words of confirmation that Jesus was the redemption in Jerusalem (Luke 2:36–38).

Jesus's ministry in both word (Matthew 4:14–17) and deed (Matthew 8:16–17) fulfilled scripture (Isaiah 9:1–2; 53:4).[5] The Pharisees accused Jesus of nullifying the law, but Jesus reassured them: "Do not think that I came to destroy the Law or the Prophets. I did not come to destroy but to fulfill" (Matthew 5:17). Jesus added, "One jot or one tittle will by no means pass from the law till all is fulfilled" (Matthew 5:18), which provides us with one of the strongest affirmations in the Bible of the inerrancy of scripture.[6]

Before Jesus appeared, many proclaimed themselves as the Messiah. Even after His death, others have tried to proclaim it, such as Theudas (Acts 5:36) or the Egyptian (Acts 21:38). The historian Josephus called both of them imposters. According to the historian Josephus, Theudas convinced his followers to leave their possessions and follow him to the Jordan River, where he promised a miracle would take place at his command, such as the river parting as it did for Moses and allowing them to cross over.[7] His followers were deceived; some were taken to prison, and others were killed. Theudas was eventually captured and beheaded on the spot.[8]

Almost the same thing happened to the Egyptian and his followers; most were taken to prison or killed. Even though this

---

[5] Brand, Draper, and England, s.v. "fulfill."

[6] Earl Radmacher, Ron Allen, and H. Wayne House, *Compact Bible Commentary* (Nashville: Thomas Nelson, 2004), 670.

[7] Rebecca Gray, *Prophetic Figures in Late Second Temple Jewish Palestine: Evidence from Josephus* (New York: Oxford University Press, 1993), 115.

[8] Gray, 115.

happened not long after the death of Jesus, it gives us a sense of how easily the same people who rejected Jesus believed others were the Messiah. Many others came professing to be the Prophet and the Messiah, but the real Jesus Christ from Nazareth performed miracles, proving He was the incarnate true God.

Mark, Matthew, Luke, and John concluded that the miracles, signs, and wonders performed by Jesus demonstrated His power, authority, and sovereignty as the Son of God. As a prophet of God, Jesus predicted His death, making His resurrection the event that birthed Christianity. In this supernatural event, God's prophetic pronouncement over the seed of the woman came to fruition.

CHAPTER TWO

THE POWER OF JESUS

And Jesus came and spoke to them, saying, "All authority
has been given to Me in heaven and on earth."
—MATTHEW 28:18

The definition of power is the ability to act or produce an effect.
The word *power* is found in the Bible more than two hundred
times. In the process of creation, God demonstrated His power.
This is why God is known as the Omnipotent; only He in the
persons of the Father, the Son, and the Holy Spirit have the
almighty power or the infinite power. In referring to Jesus, John
acknowledges the power of Jesus.

> All things were made through Him, and without
> Him nothing was made that was made. (John 1:3)

In writing to the church in Colossae, the Apostle Paul
referring to Jesus wrote:

> For by Him all things were created that are in
> heaven and that are on earth, visible and invisible,

whether thrones or dominions or principalities or
powers. All things were created through Him and
for Him. (Colossians 1:16)

Jesus demonstrated His power, and He was not afraid
to come against paradigms of His era. The Pharisees, the
Sadducees, and the scribes were very attentive to the ministry
of Jesus. It was part of their culture to inquire about anyone who
proclaimed to be a prophet, the Messiah, or who performed
miracles. They did it with John the Baptist, and John the
Baptist called them vipers. Their presence did not intimidate
Jesus. In spite of them, Jesus continued His ministry to save the
lost sheep. Many people received Jesus; others received healing.
Many people received comfort, many received miracles. And
many rejected Him.

At an early age, Jesus demonstrated that He was a remarkable
being. As the Son of Man grew, He increased in wisdom, stature,
and favor with God and men (Luke 2:52). When He was twelve
years old, Jesus demonstrated to the doctors of the law, Mary,
and Joseph that He had knowledge and understanding of the
Scriptures. They were amazed at His intelligence (Luke 2:46–47).
I certainly believe that Jesus performed extraordinary miracles
in the days of His childhood and youth. This is evident through
events such as the water being turned into wine at the wedding
in Cana of Galilee. Jesus and his disciples were invited to this
wedding, and the mother of Jesus was there too. The mother of
Jesus told him that their hosts had run out of wine. It was like
telling Jesus to do something about it. Usually, mothers are very
intuitive with their children and know them very well. Mary
knew her Son and His capabilities.

Jesus replied, "Woman, what does your concern
have to do with Me? My hour has not yet come."
(John 2:3–4)

The signs were there that Jesus had power, and Mary knew this. Jesus stated that His power was the power of God. He was not afraid to answer His enemies (John 5:17–19; John 10:28–30). Even more, the chief priests, the scribes, and the elders of Jesus's era acknowledged that Jesus had some kind of power. They asked Jesus, "By what authority are You doing these things? And who gave You this authority to do these things" (Matthew 21:23; Mark 11:28; Luke 20:2). These verses confirm that the enemies of Jesus acknowledged that Jesus had the authority and power to do extraordinary things. On another occasion, the scribes acknowledged that Jesus had the power to cast out demons (Mark 3:22; Luke 11:15). Jesus reassured them that He was casting demons out by the power of God (Luke 11:18–19).

Jesus could rebuke devils and cast out demons. However, in one instance in the Bible, the disciples were not able to cast out a demon. A man brought his son to the disciples to be free of a demon that tormented him by throwing him many times into the fire or the water. The father clearly stated that his son often was thrown into the fire or water. He knew that the demon was trying to kill his son.

It wasn't until Jesus came down from the mountain that He delivered the possessed young man (Matthew 17:15-19). So, where was Jesus when the disciples were trying to cast out the demon? Jesus had gone to the Mount of Transfiguration with Peter, James, and John.

Often, Jesus separated Himself from the crowd to pray. On this occasion, Moses and Elijah appeared to Jesus. Peter, James, and John saw the transfiguration of Jesus. Even more, Peter, James, and John knew that Jesus had spoken with Moses and Elijah. After the whole event of the transfiguration of Jesus, He cast out the epileptic spirit that tormented the possessed son.

Throughout His ministry, Jesus demonstrated power. The miracles that Jesus performed gave Him fame that He did not seek and helped many people acknowledge that he had supernatural power. Even Herod, who killed John the Baptist, heard about Jesus and His power. Herod believed that John the Baptist had risen from the dead and that John the Baptist was performing miracles (Matthew 14:2). Jesus knew He had power, but He did not boast about it. Instead, Jesus used it to glorify God. At one time, a woman came seeking healing. The woman touched His garment. Jesus looked around and asked, "Who touched my clothes?" (Mark 5:30). Jesus acknowledged that power came out of Him.

Jesus had the power to lead by example. He had the power to know the intentions of the hearts of the people. Jesus had the power to fast, pray for hours, heal the sick, call people to repent and change their ways. Jesus had the power to assemble multitudes, speak the Word of God with authority, and overcome temptation; Jesus had the power to love, forgive sins, and change people's lives.

Jesus had the power to prophesy. As a prophet, He foresaw the destruction of Jerusalem's temple, which occurred in AD 70. Jesus foretold the denial of Peter and the betrayal of Judas. Jesus had the power to teach the Word of God.

Jesus had the power of restoration. Jesus had the power to bless. Jesus had the power to be cursed for the salvation of many (Galatians 3:13). Jesus had the power of redemption. Jesus had the power to stand against false accusations and false witnesses. Jesus had the power to stand against His enemies. Jesus had the power to be hated without reason (John 15:24–25). Jesus demonstrated the power to ascend and descend. Jesus had the power to speak in parables. Jesus had the power of the priesthood. Jesus had the power of a king. Jesus had power over light and darkness. Jesus had the power of wisdom, intelligence, and science. Jesus had the power of knowledge. Jesus had the power of a shepherd. Jesus had the power of a teacher. Jesus had the power of Elijah. Jesus had the power of an intercessor.

Jesus demonstrated the power of provision. He had the power

to convert water into wine, which was one of His first miracles. Jesus had the power to speak life; it happened to the dying son of a nobleman (John 4:46). Jesus demonstrated the power to heal people, and such was the case with the man He healed at the pool of Bethesda. Jesus demonstrated the power of multiplication.

A great example is when Jesus multiplied the fishes and the bread (John 6:9-13). Jesus had the power to walk on water. Jesus had the power to heal the blind. Jesus had the power to resurrect. Even more, God has given the name of Jesus power. In teaching the disciples how to pray, Jesus said, "Whatever you ask in My name, that will I do, so that the Father may be glorified in the Son. If you ask Me anything in My name, I will do it" (John 14:13–14). This revelation is powerful because when Jesus told this revelation to the disciples, they were not praying in His name. Jesus says, "Until now you have asked nothing in My name; ask, and you will receive, so that your joy may be made full" (John 16:24).

The disciples had access to receive power in Jesus's name. For example, the disciples saw a man driving out demons on one occasion, and they tried to stop the man.

> Now John answered and said, "Master, we saw someone casting out demons in Your name, and we forbade him because he does not follow with us." But Jesus said to him, "Do not forbid him, for he who is not against us is on our side." (Luke 9:49–50)

This man grasped the teachings of Jesus quickly. This man was using the mighty name of Jesus because he realized the teachings of Jesus were true. This man was an example of how the name of Jesus would be able to be used by all who believe.

The most extraordinary power that Jesus had was that of humility. The Son of God left His glory to live among sinners and bring salvation to humanity. He did not have a place to live, but He gave His life to the ministry. Day and night, for more than three years, Jesus dwelled and interacted with His disciples, the rich, the working class, the poor, and people interested in knowing Jesus.

The opposite of humility is pride. Many people confuse confidence with arrogance. Jesus had the assurance and the certainty of His powers. Jesus knew what He had and who He was.

In giving His life to the ministry, Jesus demonstrated the power to serve:

> For even the Son of Man did not come to be served, but to serve, and to give His life a ransom for many. (Mark 10:45)

Before His death, Jesus celebrated the Passover with His disciples. Knowing that Judas would betray Him, Jesus still served the supper. Jesus also washed the disciples' feet before His betrayal to demonstrate the power of humility and servitude. Even though Jesus knew what was about to take place, Jesus maintained His godly posture and continued to do the work of God.

CHAPTER THREE

THE RESURRECTION OF JESUS

But He was wounded for our transgressions, He was bruised for our iniquities;
The chastisement for our peace was upon him, and by His stripes we are healed.

—ISAIAH 53:5

Jesus performed many miracles, and they were the prelude to His death, His resurrection, and the birth of Christianity. Jesus also prophesied of events that would lead to His rejection, His death, and His resurrection (Mark 8:31).

From a religious context, Jesus changed the paradigm because new things were about to emerge after His death. Jesus was the miracle that many were waiting for. What is a miracle? A miracle is a supernatural act of God or a special act of God that interrupts the natural course of events.[9] My definition of a miracle is an extraordinary supernatural act of God that at all times surpasses the limited mind of humanity. The resurrection of Jesus interrupted the natural course of events and the history

---

[9] Norman L. Geisler, *The Big Book of Christian Apologetics* (Grand Rapids, MI: Baker Books, 2012).

of mankind. Again, Jesus was the miracle that many were waiting for; He was the Messiah.

There is no doubt that Jesus existed. Historians such as Josephus wrote about Jesus. Josephus reported Jesus as a "worker of amazing deeds." Celsus accused Jesus of being a magician, and the Talmud said that Jesus practiced sorcery.[10]

In Jesus's time, the Pharisees and the scribes accused Jesus of casting out demons by Beelzebub, the ruler of demons (Matthew 12:24; Mark 3:22; and Luke 11:15). The Pharisees and the scribes acknowledged that Jesus had power, but they denied that it was from God. Judas betrayed Jesus, Peter denied Jesus, and other prophecies were fulfilled (Psalm 41:9; Zechariah 11:12; Isaiah 53:7; Psalm 22:1–2; Psalm 22:7–8; Psalm 22:15; and Psalm 22:17–18). Jesus was mocked, despised, and crucified with two criminals. One was on the left, and the other was on the right, leaving Jesus in the middle. Many witnessed His crucifixion.

The practice of crucifixion was used by many ancient nations such as Egypt, Assyria, Media, and Persia. It seems that originally a cross was a pointed wooden stake used to build a wall or erect fortifications around a town.[11] It is believed that idea came from the practice of hanging up bodies. Individuals would be executed on stakes and left for public display. An early example in the Bible is Genesis 40:19, where Joseph tells the chief baker that he will be hung on a tree. Another example is seen when the Philistines displayed the bodies of Saul and his sons (1 Samuel 31:8-18).

The Assyrians and Persians utilized crucifixion to display the heads of captured enemies or particularly heinous criminals. As time passed, crucifixion developed into a form of capital punishment. Enemies of the state were impaled on the stake itself. When Alexander the Great took over the city of Tyre, he

---

[10] Michael R. Licona, *The Resurrection of Jesus: A New Historical Approach* (Downers Grove, IL: InterVarsity Press, 2010), 282.

[11] Charles Brand, Charles Draper, and Archie England, *Holman Illustrated Bible Dictionary* (Nashville: Holman Bible Publishers, 2003), s.v. "crucifixion."

hung about two thousand people. As time when on, the practice did not fade away but rather continued for many centuries more. Even when Palestine was under the control of the Greeks and the Romans, many were hung. Under Alexander Jannaeus, who was the second Hasmonean king, eight hundred Pharisees were crucified. At first, the Greeks and the Romans reserved the punishment only for slaves, saying it was too barbaric for the freeborn or citizens.[12]

By the first century, however, it was used for any enemy of the Roman state, though citizens could only be crucified by the direct edict of Caesar. As time went on, the Romans began to use crucifixion more and more as a deterrent to criminal activity, so that by Jesus' time, it was a common sight.[13]

Crucifixion was a slow and painful death. Archaeological findings of gravesites prove the practice of crucifixion by the Romans. Today, there is plenty of evidence of the resurrection of Jesus. Dr. Gary Habermas and Michael Licona are experts in the case of the resurrection of Jesus:

> Five historical principles speak to Resurrection;
> Multiple independent sources support historical claims.
> Attestation by an enemy supports historical claims.
> Embarrassing admissions support historical claims.
> Eyewitness testimony supports historical claims.
> Early testimony supports historical claims.[14]

Most of the New Testament authors confirm that many eyewitnesses saw Jesus die and saw him after his resurrection.

---

[12] Charles Brand, Charles Draper, and Archie England, *Holman Illustrated Bible Dictionary* (Nashville: Holman Bible Publishers, 2003), s.v. "crucifixion."
[13] Charles Brand, Charles Draper, and Archie England, *Holman Illustrated Bible Dictionary* (Nashville: Holman Bible Publishers, 2003), s.v. "crucifixion."
[14] Gary R. Habermas and Michael R. Licona, *The Case for the Resurrection of Jesus* (Grand Rapids, MI: Kregel Publications, 2004), 39.

CELESTE PEREZ

Many of these eyewitnesses were interviewed. Luke is one of those who interviewed some of these eyewitnesses.

> Inasmuch as many have taken in hand to set in order a narrative of those things which have been fulfilled among us, just as those who from the beginning were eyewitnesses and ministers of the word delivered them to us, it seemed good to me also, having had perfect understanding of all things from the very first, to write to you an orderly account, most excellent Theophilus, that you may know the certainty of those things in which you were instructed. (Luke 1:1–4)

Other supernatural events took place, such as the appearance of Jesus to many people. There was sudden darkness covering the skies, the veil of the temple tore at that very moment of Jesus's death, an earthquake took place, many graves opened, and many saints were resurrected from their graves.

When Jesus died, the holy of holies was exposed. Before continuing, I would like to tell a little about the ark of the covenant which was housed in the holy of holies. The ark of the covenant held the presence of God. Prior to the resurrection of Jesus, the ark of the covenant was not in the temple. Yet the holy of holies was preserved by a thick veil. Many centuries before Jesus, the ark of the covenant disappeared. Many believe the Babylonians took it. Others believe it is still hidden in Jerusalem. Today, many are still puzzled about what happened to the ark of the covenant. The disappearance of the ark of the covenant is a mystery to scholars. God gave specific instructions to Moses about how to build the ark of the covenant.

The ark of the covenant was very significant because it represented the presence of God dwelling among them. It was sanctified and holy. The ark of the covenant is a chest made of gold. On the top of which are two cherubs facing each other. Cherubs are angels. One of the duties of cherubim is to protect. At the fall of man, God placed cherubim at the east side of the Garden of Eden to protect the tree of life. The golden cherubim guarded the ark of the covenant, and only those authorized, only the high priest, could enter the place of the holy of holies. Any unauthorized person would surely die. Many centuries before the death of Jesus, the ark of the covenant was in constant movement with the people of Israel. On one occasion, the Philistines took possession of it, but that brought them calamities from God. When the ark of the covenant was recovered and being brought back to Jerusalem on a oxen drawn cart the oxen stumbled. Uzzah, an unauthorized person, tried to sustain it with his hand, but he was immediately killed because he was not a high priest.

Even if the ark of the covenant was not behind the veil, the fact that the veil tore precisely at the moment of Jesus' death is a supernatural event. There is no separation between God and humanity. Now, God's presence is accessible at all times. Through Jesus, His presence is with us. Even more, He dwells in believers.

Jesus was not embalmed in the way we embalm people today. He was embalmed in the Roman style. Usually, in Israel, the bodies were cleaned, massaged with herbal oils, and wrapped in a clean sheet. In Egypt, the practice of embalming was different. They removed the blood from the bodies and used salt for preservation. Jacob and Joseph were embalmed in the Egyptian way.

Anubis was the Egyptian god of death, the god of embalming, and the god who watches the gate of death. The head of this god is shaped like a dog's face. It is interesting to note that dogs were unclean animals in Israel, and it was forbidden to sacrifice dogs as an offering. In the days of Moses, dogs were like wolves. They traveled in packs and were scavengers:

> Do not give what is holy to the dogs; nor cast
> your pearls before swine, lest they trample them

under their feet, and turn and tear you in pieces.
(Matthew 7:6)

This verse is significant because, as time progressed from its beginning until the time of Jesus, the Israelites did not preserve the holy things.

There were many more Bible stories about people in Israel showing little regard for the things of God. Many people in Israel took the things of God in vain. When Jesus tells us not to give precious things to dogs or swine, it references people who are enemies of Jesus or enemies of the gospel. Jesus had many enemies, including the Pharisees, Sadducees, scribes, chief priests, elders, and the Romans. Jesus was the Messiah, and He considered His teachings to be holy and precious like pearls or a treasure.

When someone gives you a gift, such as an expensive ring or a piece of precious jewelry, you make sure it is secured. Occasionally, it is cleaned or buffed. Usually, you will wear it because it means something to you or has some value to you. The same reasoning should be done with Jesus and His teachings. They have value for Christians.

From the trajectory of centuries, the Jews have been waiting for the Messiah. Today, many Jews are still waiting for the Messiah, but the Holy One has already come. They rejected Jesus, gave Jesus to the dogs or the swine—the Romans of that specific era—and killed Jesus. The same Romans destroyed Jerusalem in AD 70.

The existence of principalities and powers is real and biblical. One of them is death. The Egyptians and pagan countries around Israel worshipped death. The Aztecs used to worship the god of death. Today, many cultures celebrate the day of the dead. For example, the Day of the Dead is usually celebrated on the first or second of November in Mexico.

In 2001, I had a dream where a principality came flying

toward me. In my dream, I knew in my spirit that he was a principality of death. This being had the power to cause death. He was shouting, "I have the power to do this and to do that." As this principality was flying, he was approaching me. I started rebuking him in the name of Jesus and declaring, "You have no power or authority—only Jesus has the power over death." The next day, as an intern embalmer, I went to embalm a body, and to my surprise, the man on the table had the same tattoo as the principality in my dream. I couldn't believe it. God revealed to me that the church is often fighting against the principality of death. It can mean spiritual death. But I will add that many Christians have died before their time.

Jesus conquered death. There is physical death, spiritual death, and eternal death, and Jesus conquered all three! Jesus knew He was going to die under unusual circumstances. As a prophet—and as the Son of God—Jesus knew His death was going to be painful. The way Jesus died was degrading.

Usually, in old Israel, when someone brought shame to the community, that person would be stoned to death and then hung from a tree:

> For he who is hanged is accursed by God. (Deuteronomy 21:23)

According to the enemies of Jesus, He brought guilt and shame to Israel by proclaiming to be the Messiah. Yet, Jesus was doing all the signs of the Messiah. One of the hanging requirements was that the body could not be left overnight on the tree because God did not want the land to be defiled.

The pain that Jesus endured on the cross must have been unbearable. Jesus was giving birth to something very significant in the spiritual realm. Jesus never gave up. Jesus knew He had to go through this process to conquer death and bring salvation to the world. How many times have our expectations disappointed us? Israel expected the Messiah to come as a king, with an army, with status, or with influence, to prove that He was the Messiah. I imagine these were some of their thoughts:

- How can Jesus be the Savior?
- He is poor.
- He has no status.
- He has no influence.
- He was born in Bethlehem, a small town that barely makes a sound.
- He was raised in Nazareth, a town that is not even on the map!

All Jesus's enemies questioned how Jesus could be the Messiah, yet they acknowledged that He did have some kind of power.

> For My thoughts are not your thoughts, nor are your ways My ways, says the Lord. For as the heavens are higher than the earth, so are My ways higher than your ways, and My thoughts than your thoughts. (Isaiah 55:8–9)

In our Christian walk, we must ask God about His thoughts about us. I have learned to ask God about His thoughts about me. I have asked God about His ways in my life because I have ideas about me too. I have an image of how I want my life to be, but I wonder if my ways are in accord with the ways of God. Talking to God and praying for His will leads me to self-examination. King David reached out to God and said, "Examine me, O Lord, and prove me; Try my mind and my heart" (Psalm 26:2).

Jesus gave the model prayer to His disciples. Jesus encouraged His disciples to say, "Your kingdom come, Your will be done on earth as it is in heaven" (Matthew 6:10).

Jesus often struggled to accomplish God's will because of the opposition in His life and because He was a human being. He reasoned with God. Jesus often prayed alone because He knew He could not do it alone. Jesus needed the help of the Father and the Holy Spirit. Jesus uttered powerful words before His crucifixion:

> Abba, Father, all things are possible for You. Take this cup away from Me; nevertheless, not what I will, but what You will. (Mark 14:36)

Jesus's relationship with His Father is expressed in this verse. Jesus called His Father *"Abba,"* which is the Aramaic word for "Papa" or "Daddy." Yet, the Jews did not use the word *Abba* in addressing God because they felt it was disrespectful.[15]

As the unique Son of God, Jesus was on the most intimate terms with His Father. Jesus knew that His Father could do anything, and He asked that God take this cup from Him.[16] Jesus had a very close relationship with His Father. Jesus demonstrated His love for His Father and trusted His Father. Jesus was fighting a battle to do His Father's will. To do the will of the Father and to know the will of God in our lives as Jesus did, we must pray and talk to the Father.

Jesus was crucified, died, and His body was removed before nightfall. His bones were not broken, which fulfilled the scriptures (Psalm 34:20; John 19:36). It is believed that Jesus was in His thirties when He was crucified.

From His death to His reappearance, three days and three nights lapsed. Many things can happen in three days. The number three is interesting. We serve a triune God: the Father, the Son,

---

[15] Rodney L. Cooper and Max Anders, *Holman New Testament Commentary Mark* (Nashville, TN: Broadman & Holman Publishers, 2000), Mark 14:36.
[16] Rodney L. Cooper and Max Anders, *Holman New Testament Commentary Mark* (Nashville, TN: Broadman & Holman Publishers, 2000), Mark 14:36.

and the Holy Spirit! On the third day, God created the earth, the seas, and the vegetation. Joseph interpreted the dream for Pharaoh's butler, and in three days, Pharaoh restored the butler's position in the palace (Genesis 40).

In contrast, the chief baker of Pharaoh was beheaded. Joseph put his brothers in jail for three days. The Bible is full of stories where God used three days and three nights to give victory to so many characters:

- For three days, there was a thick darkness in the land of Egypt.
- God meant for the Israelites to go through the desert in three days.
- For three days, the Israelites went into the wilderness and found no water until God made the water sweet at Marah.
- Within three days, the Israelites crossed over the Jordan to possess the land.
- For three days, Rahab hid the spies.
- For three days, the Philistines could not explain the riddle of Samson.
- The donkeys of Kish, the father of Saul, were lost for three days.
- David fasted for three days and three nights.
- Esther and the Jews fasted for three days and three nights.

Mary and Joseph were looking for Jesus, and after three days, they found Him sitting in the temple with the teachers. The number three refers to completeness. Before the arrest of Jesus, He prayed three times in the garden of Gethsemane:

> He was placed on the cross at the third hour of the day (9 A.M.) and died at the ninth hour (3 P.M.). Three hours of darkness covered the land while Jesus was suffering on the cross from the

sixth hour to the ninth hour. Three is the number
of resurrection.[17]

Do you have an experience where the number three became
relevant in your life? On one occasion, God put in my heart to
pray and fast for three days and three nights. It was my first time
doing a dry fast for three days and three nights. I was excited and
not sure if I could have finished it. I expected that God would do
something about it. The thing is that God did something about
the matter, but it was not in the way I expected it. I wanted God
to intervene and prevent a decision that someone else made. God
reminded me that everyone has free will. No one can force anyone
to stop doing something when that person makes up his or her
mind to go forth—even though the decision might bring pain to
others.

During those days of prayer and fasting, God visited me. On
my second or third day, I was weak. As I was sitting on the couch
and praying to God, I closed my eyes. Suddenly, the room got
bright, and as I opened my eyes, I saw two angels in my living
room. I could tell they were talking about me. One of the angels
was pointing at me. As I am writing down this experience, my
eyes are getting watery because it was so real.

I jumped up on the couch, raised my right arm, and called out
to Jesus. I said, "Jesus, help me!" I was thrown back on the couch
and put to sleep. It felt like I was not supposed to see the angels
talking to each other about me. That experience helped me realize
that although things did not go the way I wanted them to, God
still opened my spiritual eyes to see Him working in me. Others
may choose to make decisions that hinder the family, but that does
not mean that God is not in control. God opened my spiritual eyes
to see that angels are working on our behalf. God sends angels to

---

[17] "The Meaning of the Numbers in the Bible: The Number 3," Biblestudy.org,
accessed 2020,
https://www.biblestudy.org/bibleref/meaning-of-numbers-in-bible/3.html.

protect us and guide us through complicated matters or situations. This dry fast for three days and three nights that God put in my heart to do became unforgettable. It revealed to me the experience of angelic visitations.

Jesus was dead for three days and three nights, but where was He during this time? As Matthew states Jesus was in the heart of the earth.

> For as Jonah was three days and three nights in the belly of the great fish, so will the Son of Man be three days and three nights in the heart of the earth. (Matthew 12:40)

Sheol was a place for dead people. Jesus related the story of Lazarus and a rich man. They both were in a place where they could see each other and talk to each other, but a division separated them. The rich man was in Hades also known as Sheol in the Old Testament, and Lazarus was in the bosom of Abraham referred to as paradise. Jesus was in Sheol for three days and three nights. What was Jesus doing there? The first Adam gave the kingdom of earth to Satan, and the Second Adam (Jesus) was going to retrieve the keys from Satan by overcoming death.

John had a vision of the Son of Man:

> I am He who lives, and was dead, and behold, I am alive forevermore. Amen. And I have the keys of Hades and of Death. (Revelation 1:18)

The Second Adam took the keys of Hades and death from the serpent. The Romans placed soldiers to guard the tomb of Jesus because the chief priests and the Pharisees remembered Jesus saying that He would rise in three days. They asked Pilate to place soldiers by the tomb because they were afraid the disciples would steal the body and proclaim a resurrection had taken place.

After three days, many people came forth and confirmed that the tomb of Jesus was empty. Mary Magdalene and another woman named Mary went to the tomb, but an angel had removed the stone. When the angel appeared to them, even the soldiers were scared. Jesus was not there, and while the women were following the instructions of the angel, Jesus appeared to them on their way to see the disciples. In addition, Jesus appeared to many people for forty days and nights, including two men headed to Emmaus.

Because of the death of Jesus, the disciples were shaken, scared, and in hiding. The guards ran to tell the chief priests about the appearance of the angel and the disappearance of the body of Jesus. The chief priests and elders decided to bribe the soldiers as they did with Judas. Imagine Judas in Sheol seeing Jesus retrieving the keys from the principality of Hades and Death.

Resurrection is the act of rising from the dead—the process where the decaying flesh comes back to life. The resurrection of Jesus proved that Jesus came back in a glorified body. Jesus, the incarnate of God, proved to have the power of resurrection. During His earthly ministry years, He performed miracles in which He resurrected several people, even one of His closest friends, Lazarus. Only the Son of Man has the authority to resurrect Himself from the grave.

After Jesus appeared to His disciples, they worshipped Jesus. However, Thomas was not with the disciples at this time, and when the disciples told him of the appearance of Jesus, he did not believe them:

> Unless I see in His hands the print of the nails, and put my finger into the print of the nails, and put my hand into His side, I will not believe. (John 20:25)

Thomas saw how the guards had nailed Jesus's hands and feet to the cross and how one of the guards had pierced the side of

Jesus. Jesus appeared again when all of them were together and said:

> Thomas, because you have seen Me, you have believed. Blessed are those who have not seen and yet have believed. (John 20:29)

This message is still active and alive! The resurrection of Jesus is real, it did take place, and Jesus is alive! Finally, Jesus gave the disciples instructions to stay in Jerusalem because He would be sending the Holy Spirit.

CHAPTER FOUR

THE BIRTH OF CHRISTIANITY

*But when the fullness of time had come, God sent forth
his Son, born of woman, born under the law.*

—GALATIANS 4:4

The first thing that comes to my mind when I hear the word
birth is a woman giving birth. God gave women the power
to give birth in the physical realm. I have heard many stories
of women giving birth and how painful it is. Today, with the
advancements of medical science, the pain is lessened. One of
the signs that a woman is about to give birth is groaning pains.
Even Jesus, God incarnate, compared Himself to a woman
giving birth:

> Now I will cry like a woman in labor, I will pant
> and gasp at once. (Isaiah 42:14)

Jesus was speaking to His disciples, but they did not
understand Him.

Now Jesus knew that they desired to ask him, and he said to them, "Are you inquiring among yourselves about what I said, 'A little while, and you will not see Me; and again a little while, and you will see Me'? Most assuredly, I say to you that you will weep and lament, but the world will rejoice; and you will be sorrowful, but your sorrow will be turned into joy. A woman, when she is in labor, has sorrow because her hour has come; but as soon as she has given birth to the child, she no longer remembers the anguish, for joy that a human being has been born into the world. Therefore you now have sorrow; but I will see you again, and your heart will rejoice, and your joy no one will take from you." (John 16:19–22)

But why compare Himself to a woman in labor? A woman in labor is having one of the most painful experiences, which is the act of bringing forth life. So many women have died giving birth. One example in scripture is the story of Rachel giving birth to Benjamin. The scripture says that she had a "hard labor." Like Rachel, Jesus in the Garden of Gethsemane, while praying experienced what we might called a hard labor (Matthew 26:36-46). That even Jesus said to His disciples, "My soul is exceedingly sorrowful, even to death" (Matthew 26:38). Jesus's statement is similar to the experience that women go through while in laboring which can bring them close to death. Jesus was determined to go through His death, but He took courage and strength from God.

The resurrection of Jesus shook the city of Jerusalem. It was a supernatural event. More than ever before, the disciples were comforted. This time, they were determined not to fail Jesus. They decided to stay in Jerusalem.

The Romans were trying to maintain order in the city. The chief priests were trying to figure out how to go about their duties, keep quiet about the resurrection of Jesus, and fix the inner sanctuary, the Holy of Holies. Visitors from different regions heard all types of rumors, and many were still trying to see the effects of the earthquake.

The disciples decided to obey the instructions of Jesus, stick together, and take the time to fellowship. The writings of Luke, especially the book of Acts, give specific details about the disciples waiting for the promise. The book of Acts provides us with a lot of the history of the primitive church.

The first thing they did was to be obedient to the words of Jesus. They went to Mount Olive, which is near Jerusalem, and they went into an upper room. All the disciples and followers of Jesus, including women—even Mary, the mother of Jesus—and his brothers gathered at this place. They maintained themselves in one accord in prayers and supplications. What were they praying? I believe they were praying for many things, but especially for the promise.

Jesus said they would receive power. Jesus knew they would need this power. When the power of Jesus was revealed to them, they did not grasp it. Jesus walked with them and taught them many things, but they did not understand. Through the Holy Spirit, they would be guided to the light and understand the many things that would be revealed to them, even the things that Jesus taught while He was with them.

This gathering in prayer is a sign of the birth of Christianity. The baptism of the Holy Spirit is the confirmation of the things to come. After the baptism of the Holy Spirit, the disciples were not the same. They had the power and were working in a different realm. A great example is Peter. After the baptism of the Holy Ghost, Peter, with the eleven, gave such a powerful sermon that thousands of people accepted Jesus and were added to the birthing church:

Repent, and let every one of you be baptized in
the name of Jesus Christ for the remission of sins;
and you shall receive the gift of the Holy Spirit.
(Acts 2:38)

What a simple but powerful message! It was powerful because
they had received the Holy Spirit!

This group of people birthed the primitive church, but the
resurrection of Jesus birthed Christianity. The disciples became
apostles, and Matthias replaced Judas. God gave the disciples a
promotion. No longer would they be known as disciples; they
were apostles. Through this promotion, they advanced in the
kingdom of God. The apostles even established churches for the
kingdom of God.

The new converts received the words of the apostles and their
teachings. They practiced fellowship by taking Holy Communion
and praying. Many miracles occurred; many received healing and
salvation. Soon persecution came for the apostles. Their enemies,
many of whom were Pharisees and Sadducees, had the idea that if
they could threaten, persecute, or jail them, it would prevent the
growth of this new church. But, instead, the church kept growing.

Because the apostles and the church leaders endured Satan's
persecutions, he then went to attack the church. The devil always
has a plan to destroy the work of God. The devil will try to
persecute the church leaders, and if that plan does not work, the
devil will try to persecute the church members. If the first plan
does not work, the devil already has another plan to execute.

Saul, a prestigious persecutor of the church, was going
to Damascus. He had an extraordinary encounter with Jesus.
Saul was a Roman citizen, a Pharisee, a doctor of the law, and
a persecutor of the Christians. He was taught at the feet of
Gamaliel. Saul was a bold and strong man. Saul believed he
was doing a pious thing for God by going to people's houses
and dragging men and women to prison. Even after the birth

of the church, Jesus appeared to His disciples and other people. Jesus appeared to Saul and is still appearing to people today. Saul became Paul. The church was skeptical about his conversion, and even the prophet Ananias, whom God chose to use to restore the eyesight of Saul, was skeptical. God calls and raises whomever He wishes—even if others are skeptical. God called Paul, a man who was very knowledgeable in the scriptures, to preach the gospel, build churches, and bring to light the scriptures to the Jews and Gentiles.

Paul had many opponents, and one of those groups was in the city of Corinth. Corinth is located in the south of Greece. These opponents denied the resurrection of Jesus. So, Paul asked what the point of preaching the gospel was if there was no resurrection of Jesus:

> But now Christ is risen from the dead, and has become the firstfruits of those who have fallen asleep. For since by man came death, by Man also came the resurrection of the dead. For as in Adam all die, even so in Christ, all shall be made alive. But each one in his own order: Christ the firstfruits, afterward those who are Christ's at His coming. (1 Corinthians 15:20–23)

Just like Jesus encouraged the disciples to wait for the promise of the Holy Spirit, the apostles encouraged the church to wait for the Second Coming of Jesus. The writings of the apostles are clear that there will be the Second Coming of Jesus. Jesus told His disciples to wait in Jerusalem for the promise of the Holy Spirit. They experienced the fulfillment of that promise. The disciples agreed about many things, especially that Jesus would keep His promises. In their writings, the apostles told their readers about the Second Coming of Jesus. The disciples did not know the day or the hour that the Holy Spirit would descend and baptize them. They reminded their readers that the day or the hour was unknown, but they were confident that it would happen. Many have tried to guess the timing of the Second Coming of Jesus, but Jesus did not command anyone to guess, assume, or calculate it. He wants us to be ready.

The primitive church paid a high price; many saints were persecuted, and many died as martyrs. Most of the apostles died horrendous deaths or were imprisoned for the sake of the gospel. Even after the deaths of all the apostles, history tells us that the persecution of Christians continued for centuries and is even found today. The first persecution was under Nero in AD 67. After that, there were nine other periods of persecution under the Roman Empire. These persecutions took place between AD 67 and AD 303. During these persecutions, many Christians died horrific deaths that are too graphic to mention in this book.

Many Christians gave their lives, and many were not afraid to die for the gospel. Each persecution from the primitive church until AD 303 solidified the birth of Christianity. All these persecutions helped spread the Word of God throughout the Roman Empire and around the world. The birth of Christianity is evidence of what Jesus came for and what He did. Jesus spoke of many things that Christians will endure because of the birth of Christianity, and one of them is continued persecution. Persecution helps spread the gospel of Jesus.

CHAPTER FIVE

WHERE IS THE POWER OF THE CHURCH?

*But you shall receive power when the Holy Spirit has come
upon you; and you shall be witnesses to Me in Jerusalem, and
in all Judea and Samaria, and to the end of the earth.*

—ACTS 1:8

The word *church* is found in the New King James Version 120 times and only in the New Testament. It comes from the Greek word *ekklesia*, which means an assembly of people. In Christianity the church is an assemblage of people for the purpose of worshipping God.

> And I also say to you that you are Peter, and on this rock I will build My church, and the gates of Hades shall not prevail against it. (Matthew 16:18)

When Peter received the revelation that Jesus is the Messiah, his spiritual eyes opened, and he saw that Jesus is the Christ and the Son of the living God (Matthew 16:16). Jesus was saying, "I know who you are, Peter." The phrase "on this rock" refers to the confession Peter made that Jesus Christ is the Anointed One.

Let us not forget that Peter's name was Simon. When Jesus was gathering His disciples, Andrew, the brother of Peter, saw Jesus first and understood that they had found the Messiah. Andrew went to Simon and brought him to Jesus:

> When Jesus looked at him, He said, "You are Simon the son of Jonah. You shall be called Cephas." (John 1:42)

Jesus gave Simon Peter the nickname Cephas, which means "stone" or "rock." Jesus foresaw that Peter would receive the revelation that Jesus is the Messiah.

Jesus was not saying that Peter would be the first pope. Jesus was looking at Peter for his confession:

> It is reasonable to understand Jesus' statement to mean that Peter was one rock among a rock quarry (the disciples). It was upon this quarry of disciples (cf. "living stones," 1 Pet. 2:5) and their understanding of Peter's confession that Jesus would build his church.[18]

We, the people who confess that Jesus is Lord and accept Jesus in our hearts, are the church. The church is not a building; it is an assembly of people who have repented of their sins and confessed that Jesus is Lord. We may refer to a building as a church because the church building is for the assembling of Christians, but the reality is that each of us is the church of Christ.

Peter writes that Christians are living stones, "you also, as

---

[18] Stuart K. Weber and Max Anders, *Holman New Testament: Matthew* (Nashville: Broadman & Holman Publishers, 2000), s.v. "church."

living stones, are being built up a spiritual house, a holy priesthood, to offer up spiritual sacrifices acceptable to God through Jesus Christ" (1 Peter 2:5).

> This interpretation fits with the apostle Paul's statement in Ephesians 2:19–22—that the church is "God's household, built on the foundation of the apostles and prophets, with Christ Jesus himself as the chief cornerstone. In him the whole [stone] building is joined together and rises to become a holy temple in the Lord … a dwelling in which God lives by his Spirit."[19]

In Matthew 16:18, Jesus added something powerful: the gates of Hades shall not prevail against the church. The church has been given power against the forces of evil.

Christian churches around the world are losing ground, influence, and power. One of the issues Christians are facing is the lack of unity and the clear division within councils and organizations. There are different belief systems and a lot of man-made rules. In one corner, there are the Baptists. In another corner, there are the Adventists. And in another corner, there are the Presbyterians. Then there are the Pentecostals, Mennonites, Lutherans, Methodists, Apostolic movement, and nondenominational churches. There is nothing wrong with any of these groups, but what message are we giving the world? Don't we serve the same God? Aren't we children of God?

As children of God with different personalities and traits, we must respect each other and pray for each other. Let us focus on the big picture which is preaching the gospel of Jesus and not be in a tug-of-war with one another. Let us not be like children talking negatively about each denomination or council;

---

[19] Weber and Anders, s.v. "church."

instead, let us encourage one another to preach the gospel so we may save souls from hell. God loves faithful Christians who consider themselves Adventists, Anabaptists, or members of other Christian groups. God loves true Christians who are Anglican and nondenominational. When Jesus comes back, He is not going to raise one denomination or one Christian group. When Jesus comes back, He is coming for one church, His bride, which is the body of Christ. In heaven, we are going to see true Christians from every Christian group.

The body of Christ is not in one accord. There is a division between Christians. Many churches are dead. Many pastors and Christian leaders are preaching dead messages that may be simple, but they are not powerful. Members of the church are not united or in one accord. Churches look more like social clubs. People without hope come to visit a church and leave without hope. The intention of the assembly of the saints is not meant to be a place for socializing; it is meant to be a place to seek the presence of God. Isn't the church supposed to be called the house of prayer?

It is written, "My House shall be called a house of prayer," but you make it a den of thieves. (Matthew 21:13)

In Jesus's time, many business transactions took place in the temple. Their motives were not godly. They were robbing the people of their focus on God and the intended purpose of the temple. Today, Christians are robbing God by not praying. It appears that the last function that churches are being used for today is holding prayer meetings. Many churches are open for social activities, which is not wrong, but let us not forget the intended purpose of the temple or church. As a church, we need to pray united with one accord. If the pastor says we will have a prayer night, hardly anyone will show up for the prayer meetings. Many lazy Christians are living mediocre lifestyles for Christ.

Today, many Christians present Jesus as a historical figure. They think Jesus is something from the past and is still dead. The primitive church experienced the baptism of the Holy Spirit and the speaking of tongues. Why are man-made churches proclaiming that this was only so for the primitive church? Aren't we preaching about the same Jesus? Jesus fasted. Jesus prayed. Jesus read and knew the Word. Sadly, survey data shows a decline in Bible reading among Christians.

The apostles demonstrated the same power as Jesus. Miracles happened. Why are we not walking and doing things as Jesus did? Why are Christians not doers of the Word or as Jesus did or not following Jesus's example? Jesus said, "Most assuredly, I say to you, he who believes in Me, the works that I do he will do also; and greater works than these he will do, because I go to My Father" (John 14:12).

Before ascending to the heavens, Jesus gave the Great Commission:

> And these signs will follow those who believe: In my name, they will cast out demons; they will speak with new tongues; they will take up serpents; and if they drink anything deadly, it will by no means hurt them; they will lay hands on the sick, and they will recover. (Mark 16:17–18)

How can Christians convince the world of its sin? The answer is by the demonstration of power. Luke writes to his friend in Christ, Theophilus, around 61 to 64 years after Christ. Unfortunately, there is not much history of Theophilus. Some scholars agree that he probably came from a pagan family and became the sixth bishop of Antioch. In contrast, other scholars believe that Theophilus was the high priest of Jerusalem from 37 – 41 C.E. mentioned by Josephus in his book Antiquities of the Jews. Finally, other scholars believe that Theophilus never existed, and it was a pseudonym name to protect the church or the Christians.

> Behold, I send the Promise of My Father upon you; but tarry in the city of Jerusalem until you are endued with power from on high. (Luke 24:49)

The word *endued* here means invested or clothed with power from on high. In other words, Luke was telling Theophilus that Jesus told His disciples to stay put in Jerusalem because He was giving them the dignity to operate on a different level. Even John the Baptist said to the crowd, "He will baptize you with Holy Spirit and fire" (Matthew 3:11). When God baptizes you with His Holy Spirit, God is giving you the privilege of being clothed with power. He is promoting you to operate in the spiritual realm according to His will. Our God is a God of promotion. Our God is a God that takes pleasure investing in us and clothing us with His power and glory.

About 500 years before John the Baptist and Jesus, God raised a minor prophet who prophesied great things:

> And it shall come to pass afterward that I will pour out My Spirit on all flesh; your sons and your daughters shall prophesy, your old men shall dream dreams, your young men shall see visions. And also on My menservants and on My maidservants I will pour out My Spirit in those days. And I will show wonders in the heavens and in the earth; Blood and fire and pillars of smoke. The sun shall be turned into darkness, and the moon into blood, before the coming of the great awesome day of the Lord. And it shall come to pass that whoever calls on the name of the Lord shall be saved. For in Mount Zion and in

Jerusalem there shall be deliverance, as the Lord
has said, among the remnant whom the Lord
calls. (Joel 2:28–32)

Joel's prophecy is still active today! God is still pouring out His Spirit. God is still raising prophets. God is still speaking in dreams. God is still giving visions. God is still showing His wonders in the heavens and on the earth. God is still listening to those who are calling on His name because God is still saving people.

I enjoy reading the book of Acts because I see a clear transformation. The disciples were clueless when they were walking with Jesus and only had the promise. After they received the Holy Spirit, their lives were changed forever. Peter's trade was fishing, and he denied Jesus three times. After receiving the Holy Spirit's impartation, God empowered him to preach boldly. He became one of the leaders of the early church.

When the disciples received the Holy Spirit, they preached with boldness, authority, courage, and fearlessness. Luke mentioned this to Theophilus in Acts 4:13:

Now when they saw the boldness of Peter and
John, and perceived that they were uneducated
and untrained men, they marveled. And they
realized that they had been with Jesus.

What many Christians lack today is the empowerment of the Holy Spirit. Many have not been with Jesus and do not have the impartation of the Holy Spirit. One can tell when someone has a relationship with Jesus and is walking with Jesus. Once a Christian receives the baptism of the Holy Spirit, he or she is transformed. The person of the Holy Spirit is real and is available to those who call upon God.

The Holy Spirit plays a huge role. First of all, the Holy Spirit convicts the world of sin (John 16:7–11). This conviction leads mankind to repentance which leads to salvation. The Holy Spirit is our helper (John 14:26). The Holy Spirit is our guide. Jesus said, "But when the Spirit of truth comes, he will guide you to the whole truth" (John 16:13).

The Holy Spirit will guide us to the whole truth and will reveal the truth. When we read the Word of God, for instance, the Holy Spirit helps us understand the Word. By knowing the truth, we shall be made free (John 8:32). The Holy Spirit gives Christians gifts such as the word of wisdom; the word of knowledge, faith, the gifts of healings, the working of miracles, and prophecy; discerning of spirits; different kinds of tongues; and the interpretation of tongues (1 Corinthians 12:8–11). Paul writes to the Galatians and reminds the church that the Holy Spirit in us produces fruit such as love, joy, peace, patience, kindness, goodness, faith, meekness, and temperance (Galatians 5:22–23).

Who can receive the gifts of the Holy Spirit? Who can receive the power of the Holy Spirit? These gifts are not for the world. These gifts were given to the early church, and these gifts are still valid for all Christians in the world. The gifts, fruit, and power are for the church of today—for all who want it.

When the disciples asked Jesus to teach them how to pray, Jesus gave them the model prayer. Jesus encouraged them to ask, to seek, and to keep knocking:

> How much more will your heavenly Father give the Holy Spirit to those who ask Him. (Luke 11:13)

The Holy Spirit is given to the children of God. Therefore, to receive power, Christians must ask God for the infilling of the Holy Spirit.

If we have the Holy Spirit, where is the power? Where is the power of Christians? Where is the power of the church? What is happening with the church today? The gifts of the Holy Spirit, the fruit of the Holy Spirit, and the power of the Holy Spirit are for this time as well. How can we preach Jesus without a demonstration and without power? One of the demonstrations that God gives to Christians is the power of the Holy Spirit. Because the Holy Spirit gave this power to the primitive church, it reached many lives. Because of this power, many people were healed, released from satanic oppression, and restored. The primitive church performed countless signs and wonders.

When people see the power of the Holy Spirit, they cannot resist. They want to be part of it because they are convinced by the power of the Holy Spirit. When I was about eight or nine years old, my church decided to have forty days and forty nights of fasting and prayer. The church was asking God for the impossible. I went down to the basement, and most of the elders were praying. As I was praying fervently, an elderly woman touched my back and started praying for me and with me. I was asking God to baptize me with the Holy Spirit, and I received the baptism of the Holy Spirit that night. I was crying with pure joy because I had received the baptism of the Holy Spirit. The baptism of the Holy Spirit is real, and God can baptize adults and children as well.

In 1996, my family and I went to Pensacola, Florida, to a revival. As we entered the church, I felt the fresh presence of God. The glory of God was in that place. There was something different in the atmosphere. I could smell something different in the air. The church was on fire for God, and the Holy Spirit was touching people, changing people, and giving them power.

That also happened in 1906 with the Azusa revival in California. It only took one man to start the fire of God. William J. Seymour asked God to show up just as He had for the primitive church. He had read about it many times, but he wanted to experience the Holy Spirit. William J. Seymour had a divine experience, and his hunger led him to seek God like never before.

Seymour asked, "God, what can I do?"
The revelation he received is that he needed to pray more:

> There are better things to be had in spiritual life, but they must be sought out with faith and prayer.[20]

Seymour went from praying five hours a day to seven hours a day:

> God give me what Parham preached, the real Holy Ghost and fire with tongues and love and power of God like the apostles had.[21]

After several years of praying, God unleashed the blessings from above—and the Holy Spirit was manifested.

God is still seeking men and women who are willing to seek God like never before. God is still seeking men and women who are willing to pay the price and let go of the worldly things that can hinder us or detain us from moving forward in Christ. God is still calling men and women who are willing to accept their callings and enter into the dimension of demonstration of power.

Christians from around the world, I say to you, as Paul said to the Romans, "Do not be conformed to this world" (Romans 12:2). Do not live a mediocre life for Christ when God has given us power against the enemy. The enemy has made many Christians spiritually dead, asleep, tired, or fatigued. Like never before, we must seek God and regain the demonstration of power to bring salvation to the souls that need Jesus.

---

[20] John G. Lake, *Spiritual Hunger, The God-Men, and Other Sermons* (Dallas: Christ for the Nations, 1982), 14.
[21] Lake, 14.

Many Christians have experienced the demonstration of power, but they are no longer operating in this dimension of power due to changes or other factors. Nevertheless, God is calling us back to operate in this dimension because these are the end times. Without the demonstration of this power, the church will not advance. Therefore, we must show the power of God.

CHAPTER SIX

A COMMON EVIL
AMONG CHRISTIANS

There is an evil which I have seen under the
sun, and it is common among men.

—ECCLESIASTES 6:1

Some scholars believe King Solomon wrote the book of Ecclesiastes because, in Ecclesiastes 1:12, the author says, "I, the Preacher, was king over Israel in Jerusalem." According to Daniel Estes,

> The book of Ecclesiastes presents itself as the words of "Qohelet" (1:1), a term that is not a personal name but rather is a descriptive title. In the epilogue of the book, "Qohelet" is preceded by the definite article (12:8), and this individual is called a "wise man" (ḥākām) in 12:9.[22]

---

[22] Daniel J. Estes, *Handbook on the Wisdom Books and Psalms* (Grand Rapids: Baker Academic, 2005), 271.

These clues, together with similar grammatical constructions that are elsewhere used to indicate an office (cf. Ezra 2:55, 57; Neh. 7:59), suggest that the author envisioned in this book is a teacher who has convened people in order to instruct them.[23]

We can agree that the book of Ecclesiastes is full of wisdom, and the author of this book spoke words that resonate with past generations, the present generation, and future generations.

Even though I am in my prime years as I write this book, like the wise man who wrote Ecclesiastes, I have seen an evil. This evil is within Christian communities. How can the church or Christians win souls for Christ when their testimonies are not in accord with God's Word? I have seen evil in the churches where leaders or pastors are not living what they preach. I have seen evil on this earth when newspapers allege that pastors or leaders are stealing money from their churches. How can the members of a church trust the leaders of the church? I have seen evil when church members engage in politics in the church and cause division.

When the devil is the fabricator of divisions, he tries to destroy the work of God. I have seen Christians fighting for positions in the church. I have seen members competing with each other to see who can sing better or preach better. Instead of saying, "Wow, what a song" or "what preaching," Christians should be saying, "God spoke to me through the preaching [or songs]."

I have seen pastors preaching God's Word from the altar to manipulate church members instead of the Holy Spirit working with the members. The altar is not for throwing darts or manipulating. The altar is there to seek the presence of God, to preach the Word of God, to teach, and to worship God. Leaders of the church must lead by example.

---

[23] Estes, 271.

I see a common evil among Christians: a lack of understanding, love, empathy, and compassion. When I was diagnosed with cancer, I was stunned when those whom I thought would be there for me, especially Christian friends and families, were not. As I met other people who were going through hard times, they told me similar stories. So many were indifferent to their situations or the hard process. These were Christian folks who professed to be followers of Christ. There is a spirit of indifference within the Christian community. It includes indifference toward the Word of God, toward our brothers and sisters in Christ, and the world. Too many Christians are consumed with themselves. Many are lovers of themselves, and many do not have the time to do good for others.

I have seen evil within families. I have seen non-Christian families give better testimony of healthy family relationships than Christian families who are raising their children in dysfunctional environments. Even though there are dysfunctional families everywhere, I am saying that I have seen nonbelievers' families doing things right and giving testimony that they are healthy, united families. Unfortunately, some pastors and ministry leaders put their ministry before their own families. God should be first, the family second, and the ministry next:

> But if anyone does not provide for his own, and especially for those of his household, he has denied the faith and is worse than an unbeliever. (1 Timothy 5:8).

Parents not having loving, open communication with their children causes great heartache within their families. I have seen Christian parents trying to get rid of their children. Parents are acting more like dictators instead of demonstrating the love of God with their children. Parents are too strict and are suffocating their children. Parents are manipulating their children's futures instead of seeking God for their children's futures.

Parents should seek the presence of God for guidance about the right time for their children to leave the nest. Many teenagers and young adults are not ready to leave the nest; many times, there are challenges or difficulties that they cannot handle. I have seen godly young adults taken out of their homes at an early age when they are unprepared and unequipped to face the world by themselves. Many young Christians had made significant mistakes in their lives because they left their homes when it was not time to leave. It opened the door for the enemy to enter and destroy their futures. The devil knows that God has a purpose for Christian girls and boys. The devil will always try to prevent Christians from reaching their prophetic calling.

I have seen an evil where people put themselves into the ministry without the calling of God, without preparation, without a covering, or without the blessing of God. It is scary but real! The calling of God is a serious matter because the salvation of souls is at stake. How many people have left the church due to uncalled, unprepared, or unblessed leaders? The ministry is a serious matter, and it represents the kingdom of God on earth.

I have seen an evil where Christians visit the sick, but the devil opens the door for gossiping. Gossiping has destroyed families. Gossiping has divided churches around the world. I have seen an evil where Christian leaders talk negatively about other ministries. Gossiping and talking negatively about other people or ministries is like practicing witchcraft.

Words are very powerful. By His words, God created, and if we are created in God's image, then our words are very powerful:

> Death and life are in the power of the tongue, and
> those who love it will eat its fruit. (Proverbs 18:21)

Every Christian should understand this concept. Our words affect our lives. Every negative word we speak against a brother or sister in Christ can affect them. But every bit of gossip or negative word spoken to a woman or man of God who stand on the Word of God will not prosper:

> Surely he shall deliver you from the snare of the fowler and from the perilous pestilence. He shall cover you with His feathers, and under his wings you shall take refuge; His truth shall be your shield and buckler. You shall not be afraid of the terror by night, nor of the arrow that flies by day, nor of the pestilence that walks in darkness, nor of the destruction that lays waste at noonday. (Psalm 91:3–6)

I have seen an evil where Christians expect evil instead of expecting good and doing good. On one occasion, Christ Jesus tells His disciples this truth:

> Do not think that I came to bring peace on earth. I did not come to bring peace but a sword. For I have come to set a man against his father, a daughter against her mother, and a daughter-in-law against her mother-in-law; and a man's enemies will be those of his own household. He who loves father or mother more than Me is not worthy of Me. And he who loves son or daughter more than Me is not worthy of Me. And he who does not take his cross and follow after Me is not worthy of Me. He who finds his life will lose it, and he who loses his life for My sake will find it. (Matthew 10:34–39)

This verse is a reality for many Christian families.

I have seen evil among Christians. The divorce rate is high, and division is the portion for so many Christian families. There is barely any distinction between the divorce rate in the world and in Christian communities. I have seen how addictions have divided Christian homes. I have seen family members disparage other family members. Isn't God powerful enough to change the hearts of people? If Christians know that Matthew 10:34-39 is a reality, why do they not ask God for wisdom to face their families' challenges?

Christians expect evil from their households instead of looking at their family members in the way God sees them. Why expect evil instead of focusing on godly things? Many Christian families are divided and are giving a bad testimony to the world. How can we win families for Christ when our own families are divided by strife, resentment, or hatred? The God we preach or teach is the only one who can bring healing and restoration to the family. Let us then meditate, pray, decree, and declare Malachi 4:6 over our Christian families so we can testify to the world that God is a God of healing and restoration:

> And he shall turn the hearts of the fathers to the children, and the hearts of the children to their fathers, lest I come and strike the earth with a curse.

I have seen a common evil among Christians. How many sons and daughters of pastors have left Christianity to serve the devil? I have seen so many Christian artists and singers who once served God but who now sing for the world. So, many have left Christian homes broken and discouraged with no return possible. As a result, there are countless numbers of people who have wound up in Hell due to the common evil among Christians. It is time for Christians to seek God like never before. Today is the day to acknowledge our faults, repent as the whole body of Christ, and seek the presence of God. Only God can help us triumph and give us the wisdom to handle difficult matters within the church.

CHAPTER SEVEN

AWAKE

Awake, you who sleep.
—EPHESIANS 5:14

The opposite of being awake is being asleep. Sleeping is necessary for the physical body because the body can heal, rest, and rejuvenate during sleep. For humans to function properly, we need sleep. In this chapter, I am talking about spiritual sleep. Spiritual sleep is not being alert to God's things and being more focused on the things of the world. The Greek word ἐγείρω translated as *awake* is found in the New King James Version roughly about 43 times. This translation of *awake* in Ephesians 5:14 means to rise or to get up. Someone who is spiritually sleeping cannot be vigilant or alert.

When Paul wrote to the Ephesians, he was in prison. Paul had several concerns about the Christians in Ephesus. Since there was no unity, Paul encouraged them to walk in unity:

> Beseech you to walk worthy of the calling with which you were called, with all lowliness and gentleness, with longsuffering, bearing with one another in love, endeavoring to keep the unity of

the Spirit in the bond of peace. There is one body and one Spirit, just as you were called in one hope of your calling; one Lord, one faith, one baptism; one God and Father of all, who is above all, and through all, and in you all. (Ephesians 4:1–6)

Since there was no unity, there was division. Each person did his or her own thing. Where there is division, there is a trace of the devil. Division opens the doors for contention, dissension, gossip, hatred, jealousy, selfish ambition, strife, and outbursts of wrath (Galatians 5:19–20).

When Christians are doing their own thing, it does not keep the unity of the Spirit for the benefit of God's calling. Christians may go to church on Sunday or any other day of the week, but that does not mean they are in unity. Christians are not in the unity of the Holy Spirit or the bonds of peace. The lack of unity is how the devil has many sleeping. Another concern Paul had with this church was the lack of love. If there is no unity, no peace, and no love, please do not call yourself a Christian. John writes to the church of Ephesus, "I have this against you, that you have left your first love" (Revelation 2:4).

Do you remember your first love? Your full attention or your undivided focus was on that specific person. You would do anything to please that person. You would sacrifice your time and energy for that love. You would care for and protect that person. The Christians in Ephesus had their attention on the world. The same is happening today with many churches. Their first love for Christ is not there, and their attention is on the world's things.

Many Christians are sleeping and need to wake up. Their attention is placed more on worldly things than on Christ. Many Christian families barely sit together to eat, pray, or read the Bible. Christians hardly go to church because they are working overtime to try to pay off credit cards. After all, there is no control in shopping. There is no discipline in wanting things. There is a difference between wanting something and needing something. Christians need two or three jobs just to make it.

Work is part of life, but God's timing is important as well. From taking the kids to sports, working, going to school, and going to medical appointments, the attention of many Christians is out of balance and not on God. I am not saying that these things are bad, but it is all about doing a reality check. Too many Christians profess to be Christians but are sleeping with their own agendas. Where is God in your daily plan? Where is God in your regular schedule?

The reality of so many Christians is that they are spiritually sleeping. There is a lack of praying, fasting, reading the Word, and congregating, and a lack of unity, peace, and love, all of which can lead to spiritual sleep. Today, there is so much entertainment from the enemy that many Christians are sleeping. I am not saying that entertainment is bad, but do not put other things before God. There are twenty-four hours in a day, and the tithes of our time should be two hours and forty minutes. In two hours and forty minutes, we can pray, read the Word, or sing to God. It is most important to have communion with God.

The book of Judges relates a remarkable story of a woman named Deborah. Her name means "bee" or "wasp." The Canaanites oppressed the Israelites for 20 years, and in despair, they cried out to God. Deborah was a prophetess and a judge and held an influential seat in her community. God gave Deborah two crucial positions in her era: she was married and probably had a family. This woman wore several hats, but she was not a complainer. God gave Deborah the wisdom to judge and the words to speak on His behalf. The scriptures say that she would sit under a palm tree, and people would come up to her with their matters. They would listen to her judgment. Deborah was a respected woman in her community.

She called Barak and instructed him to go against their enemies, but Barak lacked courage. Barak means "lightning" or "lightning flash." Barak believed the word of the prophetess, but he was not sure of his capabilities. Barak asked the prophetess to go to the battle with him, and Deborah did not hesitate. I can imagine Deborah telling her husband and family that she was going to support Barak and the battle. We do not know if her husband hesitated, but we do know that he agreed.

Barak, like a lightning flash, and Deborah, awake like a bee, went against King Jabin of Canaan. Jabin means "whom God observes." While King Jabin was oppressing the people of Israel, God was watching his life and his actions taken against the Israelites. Not even his commander-in-chief, Sisera, could prevent the prophetic words of Deborah from coming to fruition. Victory became evident for Deborah, Barak, and Israel:

> Awake, awake, Deborah! Awake, awake, sing a song. (Judges 5:12).

The word *awake* in Judges 5:12 is עוּר in Hebrew, which is the idea of opening the eyes. Even more, it is the idea of rousing oneself. It only takes one person to decide to awaken so others may join in the pursuit of the will of God. I pray that this book is a Deborah for many Christians around the world. I pray that this book becomes a Deborah and awakens the reader's spirit unto God.

Today's church is facing many challenges. Globally, the church is divided. The church is divided over political views. Christians need to pray for all leaders, even if we do not agree with their political views. The beauty of living in a democratic country is that we have the freedom to vote for the leaders who stand with God's Word:

> Therefore I exhort first of all that supplications, prayers, intercessions, and giving of thanks be made for all men, for kings and all who are in

authority, that we may lead a quiet and peaceable life in all godliness and reverence. (1 Timothy 2:2)

We live in critical times, and the Word of God is questioned all the time. That which the scripture considers evil, the world sees as good. Today, many lawmakers try to make sin a good thing or permissible thing. What is the will of God for the church of today? The intention of God for the church is to wake up.

Wake up! Can't you hear and see the signs of the end-times?

For many will come in My name, saying, "I am the Christ," and will deceive many. And you will hear of wars and rumors of wars. See that you are not troubled; for all these things must come to pass, but the end is not yet. For nation will rise against nation, and kingdom against kingdom. And there will be famines, pestilences, and earthquakes in various places. All these are the beginning of sorrows. Then they will deliver you up to tribulation and kill you, and you will be hated by all nations for My name's sake. And then many will be offended, will betray one another, and will hate one another. Then many false prophets will rise up and deceive many. And because lawlessness will abound, the love of many will grow cold. But he who endures to the end shall be saved. And this gospel of the kingdom will be preached in all the world as a witness to all the nations, and then the end will come. (Matthew 24:5–14).

Awake! Awake! Awake! Surely the signs are here. This end-time is not the time to be spiritually sleeping but the time to be awakened. There is no time to be lukewarm; it is time to seek God.

There is no time to go back; it is time to go forward and advance. We have not learned to appreciate the freedom we have. We live in a country whose foundation is built on Christianity. America is more confused than ever. When I was growing up, prayers were allowed in school. Today, in schools, not only the celebration of Halloween is more acceptable than a Christian prayer, but in some school districts, after-school Satan clubs are lawfully permitted in direct contrast to Christian good news clubs.

What about the topic of homosexuality? Christians are divided about this topic. Many argue that Jesus never preached about the topic of homosexuality. In reality, the Mosaic Law condemned homosexuality, so it was already known among the Jews what God's perception of homosexuality was. Therefore, it needed not be addressed. Pastors are afraid to preach the truth about this topic. Sadly, denominations are divided due to the issue of homosexuality. Awhile back I went to a Christian retreat and met a very discouraged pastor. She was discouraged because her denomination was divided on the subject of homosexuality. One part of her denomination held the biblical view that homosexual behaviors are abominations to God. The other part of her denomination held the world view that any sexual acts with any person are acceptable. The Bible tells Christians to love all; this includes homosexual, transsexual, and transgender people because Jesus died for all. True Christians preach what the Word says, and that is that homosexual indulgences are a sin.

> What, then, of the argument that Jesus never addressed homosexual practice and, if it had been so important, He would have addressed it clearly? Well, we've already seen that the reason the Bible doesn't speak a lot about homosexuality is because the Bible is a heterosexual book from beginning to end, and only heterosexual relationships are

sanctioned by God and only heterosexual marriage is ordained by God.[24]

Isn't the church already being persecuted about the topic of homosexuality? Awake! Awake! Awake!

I pray that the spirit of Deborah will awaken those who are sleeping. I pray that the spirit of Deborah will awaken those who lack unity, love, and peace. I pray that the spirit of Deborah will awaken the sleeping prophets, and they begin to prophesy again. I pray that the spirit of Deborah will take over the altar. I pray that pastors will awaken to preach the Word of God without compromising the Word of God. You cannot remain asleep because you will not make it. You should be either hot or cold; the Bible says you will be spat out if you are lukewarm. I pray that God would call Deborahs to awaken the apostles, prophets, evangelists, pastors, teachers, worshippers, missionaries, and intercessors in these critical times. The voice of God is saying, "Awake! Awake! Awake!"

---

[24] Michael L. Brown, *Can You Be Gay and Christian?* (Lake Mary, FL: Charisma House Book Group, 2014), 139.

CHAPTER EIGHT

ARISE

Arise from the dead.
—EPHESIANS 5:14

After many years of persecution against Christians by the Roman Empire, God intervened. Emperor Constantine had a vision of Christ, which led to his conversion to Christianity. Constantine signed the Edict of Milan (AD 313), which allowed the Roman Empire to accept all religions, including Christianity. Eventually, Christianity became the primary religious practice of Rome. Christians were finally able to enjoy freedom in Rome. However, doesn't history kind of repeat itself? Didn't many Christians come to America to escape the persecution in Europe? Unfortunately, that peace did not last long. The Goths and the Vandals persecuted the Christians. The Goths called themselves Christians, but they were actually Arians.

The Arians came from Arius of Alexandria, who was declared a heretic from the Council of Nicaea in AD 325. Arius believed that God the Father, the Son, and the Holy Spirit were separate unequal entities. Therefore, he did not accept 1 John 5:7:

For there are three that bear witness in heaven; the Father, the Word, and the Holy Spirit; and these three are one.

When Arius had another chance to speak on his beliefs, he passed away. Kaatz gives a brief description of the death of Arius.

Athanasius wrote a letter to Serapion, a fellow bishop in Egypt, claiming that Arius's death was partly the result of Bishop Alexander's prayer. Sozomen states that Arius died on the toilet where he sat, and that later no one would use the same seat. His death caused panic among the supporters of Arius, including Eusebius of Nicomedia. Some say an act of God caused Arius to die on that day, which was another way of saying that God disagreed with the Arian position. Although one might expect that with the death of Arius the Arian movement would have died along with him, this was not the case at all: if anything, Eusebius of Nicomedia became more active in trying to replace the Nicene bishops with Arian bishops.[25]

Today, there are still traces of Arianism. The heresy of Arius is active through Jehovah's Witnesses, which "deny the equality of Jesus Christ with God the Father, and hence, the Triune deity."[26] But why bring historical facts to the church of today? Today, many false teachers proclaim to be followers of Christ, but they are far from the truth of God's Word. Why is Christian history important? The church must understand its origin and

---

[25] Kevin W. Kaatz, *Early Controversies and the Growth of Christianity* (Santa Barbara: Praeger, 2012), 112.
[26] Walter Martin, *The Kingdom of the Cults* (Bloomington, MN: Bethany House, 2019), 115.

AWAKE CHRISTIANS!

purpose and be prepared to go against false teachings that distract Christians from the truth of the scriptures. How can we explain the Trinity to nonbelievers?

- "Water is one but is known in three ways: liquid, solid, and steam.
- The sun is one, but it has three kinds of main rays: light, heat, and energy.
- The air we breathe is the combination of three main gases: oxygen, nitric oxide, and carbon dioxide.
- Man is triune: spirit, soul, and body.
- The body is composed of three elements: flesh, bone, and blood."[27]

There are more examples, but I think the reader gets the picture. Looking at how God created the human body confirms that humans are created in the image of God. True Christians believe and accept that God, Jesus, and the Holy Spirit are three in one, working together in unity, but each having their distinctiveness.

The invasion of Rome—or the Sack of Rome—took place in 410. Unfortunately, many Romans blamed the Christians because they believed that this calamity was due to the acceptance of Christianity. Satan will always blame Christians and Israelites for the evil in the world. Even more, Satan twists the truth of God's Word. In Rome, there was a time when Christians were blamed for everything—even for being poor. Saint Augustine made that clear in his book entitled, *The City of God.*

Roman persecution caused many Christians to renounce the faith. However, those Christians that endured persecution and kept the faith were examples that caused many pagans to convert to Christianity. Before Rome became a Christian city, the Romans

[27] Luis M. Ortiz, *Biblical Instructions for the Newly Converted* (Santa Fe, Bogota: Ediciones Antropos LTDA, 1994), 12.

sacked many cities and temples. In his writings, Augustine asked the Christians in Rome not to focus their attention on the city of Rome. Nevertheless, to focus on the celestial city of God that is waiting for Christians. Augustine assured the Christians and saints that they did not lose anything in the sack of Rome.

Augustine said that salvation was more important than ending up in hell:

> Did they lost all they had. Their faith? Their godliness? The possessions of the hidden man of the heart, which in the sight of God are of great price? Did they lose these? For these are the wealth of Christians, to whom the wealthy apostle said, "Godliness with contentment is great gain. For we brought nothing into this world, and it is certain we can carry nothing out. And having food and raiment, let us be therewith content. But they that will be rich fall into temptation and a snare, and into many foolish and hurtful lusts, which drown men in destruction and perdition. For the love of money is the root of all evil; which, while some coveted after, they have erred from the faith, and pierced themselves through with many sorrows."[28]

In many countries around the world, persecution is a reality for Christians. Many of our enemies are being established in high places to make decisions against what Christians stand for, the Bible, God's Word.

In his final words to Timothy, Paul encourages Timothy to live what he preaches:

[28] William Edgar and K. Scott Oliphint, *Christian Apologetics: Past and Present* (Wheaton, IL: Crossway Books, 2009), 270.

But you have carefully followed my doctrine, manner of life, purpose, faith, longsuffering, love, perseverance, persecutions, afflictions, which happened to me at Antioch, at Iconium, at Lystra—what persecutions I endured. And out of them all the Lord delivered me. (2 Timothy 3:10–11)

Paul warns Timothy to expect to be persecuted:

Yes, and all who desire to live godly in Christ Jesus will suffer persecution. But evil men and impostors will grow worse and worse, deceiving and being deceived. (2 Timothy 3:12–13)

Paul never pushed back, gave up, or quit.

Day and night, the devil is trying to silence the saints' mouths so the work of the Lord will not continue.

God rouses the spirits of men and women. He has done so in the past, He is doing it in the present, and He will continue to do so until Jesus comes back. God roused the spirit of Martin Luther in 1517. While reading his Bible, Martin Luther realized that many practices in his era were not biblical. God inspired Martin Luther to write *The Ninety-Five Theses*. Many people did not know how to write or read in his time. The common people did not have access to Bibles, but Martin Luther was able to publish and make copies because the printing press had been invented, which made the printed Bible more accessible. He was persecuted for this. Many men and women have left footprints for us Christians to keep the legacy going and keep sharing the gospel so others may know Jesus and may know the truth.

How can the church arise from a state of lethargy, fatigue, and tiredness? Use the scriptures! One of my concerns is that Christians are not reading their Bibles. Today, like never before, there is easy accessibility to the Bible. Still, many Christians are not reading their Bibles, which is causing them to become illiterate of the scriptures. It is scary that so many Christians are ignorant of the Bible.

Paul encourages Timothy to use the scriptures:

> All Scripture is given by inspiration of God, and is profitable for doctrine, for reproof, for correction, for instruction in righteousness, that the man of God may be complete, thoroughly equipped for every good work. (2 Timothy 3:16–17).

Christians who do not read the scriptures are setting themselves up to fail as Christians.

Knowledge of the Word of God is powerful and spiritual. You want to become spiritual and read, know, and memorize the scriptures. Immerse yourself in the Word of God and see yourself grow. I have read so many articles about how illiterate Christians confuse characters and stories in the Bible. It is a problem, and it is an embarrassment. How can we share the gospel if we don't know our Bibles? How can we defend Christ if we do not immerse ourselves in the Word of God? Apostles, pastors, teachers, and leaders of the church must preach and teach the Word of God as intended.

Paul encourages Timothy:

> I charge you therefore before God and the Lord Jesus Christ, who will judge the living and the dead at His appearing and His kingdom: Preach the word! Be ready in season and out of season. Convince, rebuke, exhort, with all longsuffering and teaching. For the time will come when they will not endure sound doctrine, but according to their own desires, because they have itching ears,

they will heap up for themselves teachers; and they will turn their ears away from the truth, and be turned aside to fables. But you be watchful in all things, endure affliction, do the work of an evangelist, fulfill your ministry. (2 Timothy 4:1–5)

Before someone decides to arise, they must decide to follow through on the thought of arising. After their decision is firm, they can arise. God is calling His people to arise, but God cannot make that decision for His people. Christians must make the decision to arise from spiritual sleep, spiritual ignorance, and spiritual discomfort. What are you feeding your spirit? When trials come, the Word of God is going to get you through them— not the worldly things or worldly distractions.

When Jesus experienced temptations, Jesus declared the Word of God. The scripture is a powerful tool that Christians have, but many are not taking advantage of it. Many go to church to receive the Word on Sundays, but they are not reading it. Many are complacent about hearing the preaching and teaching on Saturdays or Sundays. There are no personal revelatory experiences with the scriptures. The scriptures are full of revelation. God desires to give new revelation to His people, but if Christians are not reading their Bibles, it is unlikely that revelation will come.

God has spoken to me in my dreams ever since I can remember. I usually try to write them down in my journal so I will not forget, and I pray about them and allow God to bring revelation. On May 23, 2014, God gave me a dream in which I was walking down the hallway toward the living room. There was a mirror stand and a decorative table below the mirror in the living room. When I reached the mirror in the dream, I was hoping to see my reflection. To my surprise, my reflection was not there. Jesus was reflected in the mirror. He was bright, and light emanated all over from Him. He was pointing to a Bible on the table in the dream.

The Lord said, "There is depth in my Word." When I got up, I prayed to God about the dream. The Lord told me that there is depth in His scriptures to those who are willing to seek it.

Arise, Christians, and know the scriptures, use the scriptures, and preach the scriptures. Allow the Word of God to do the work in you. Arise, apostles, and fulfill your ministry. Arise, pastors, and fulfill your ministry. Arise, teachers, and fulfill your ministry. Arise, evangelists, and fulfill your ministry. Arise, prophets, and fulfill your ministry. Arise, men and women of God, and fulfill your ministry in the name of Jesus.

Purpose in your heart to arise and fulfill your calling. Press toward the will of God in your life. Maybe you are the next president of your nation. Perhaps you are the next one God will rouse and use powerfully. Through you, many will be blessed. Through your shared testimony, many will be saved. Through your stories, many will be restored. Through you, many will receive healing. You will not know what God has in store for you until you arise. You will not see the victories until you arise. You will not conquer the land or your dreams until you arise.

CHAPTER NINE

SHINE

And Christ will give you light.
—EPHESIANS 5:14

How can Christians shine in this corrupt world? By being doers of the Word of God! The psalmist said, "Your word is a lamp to my feet, and a light for my path" (Psalm 119:105).

In the beginning, God said, "Let there be light" (Genesis 1:3). Everything was good, but through sin, darkness became the ruling force here on earth. Today, darkness is still around us, but Christ has given us back the power against the darkness. Day and night, Christians around the world are being attacked, oppressed, marginalized, afflicted, persecuted, belittled, or experiencing injustice. Still, as doers of the scripture, the darkness will never overpower the light of God.

As Christians follow and do the Word of God, God brings light into their lives. Many times, we have to make decisions. And as we walk in accord with the scriptures, God will light which way to go or which decision to make. In challenging matters, God will bring light to the situation through the Word of God. I have experienced it personally. Many times, a challenge will arise out of nowhere. As I deepen in my understanding of the Bible and seek God for guidance, God brings light, and I can see clearly what I need to do or what decision I need to make.

A great example is Moses. When Moses came down from the mountain, the people of Israel noticed that Moses's face shone (Exodus 34:29–35). Moses's shining face came to be because he was in the presence of God, and God gave him the two tablets of testimony. As one reads the Word of God, one is enlightened. Through the Word of God, wisdom, knowledge, and intelligence are imparted by God. The Word of God shapes believers to be the men or women who God intended them to be. Even more, it shapes the ministry. As one reads the Bible, our faith is lifted high. Inside, we become stronger in Christ Jesus. As Christians stand on the Word of God, mountains become valleys—and valleys become mountains—because there is power in reading God's Word.

James, in his letter, exhorts Christians to be doers of the Word:

> But be doers of the word, and not hearers only, deceiving yourselves. For if anyone is a hearer of the word and not a doer, he is like a man observing his natural face in a mirror; for he observes himself, goes away, and immediately forgets what kind of man he was. But he who looks into the perfect law of liberty and continues in it, and is not a forgetful hearer but a doer of the work, this one will be blessed in what he does. (James 1:22–25)

These verses correlate with what Jesus was telling His disciples:

> Nor everyone who says to Me, Lord, Lord, shall enter the kingdom of heaven, but he who does the will of My Father in heaven. (Matthew 7:21)

In reading the scriptures, God reveals to us His will for our lives:

> Therefore whoever hears these sayings of Mine, and does them, I will liken him to a wise man who built his house on the rock: and the rain descended, the floods came, and the winds blew and beat on that house; and it did not fall, for it was founded on the rock. But everyone who hears these sayings of Mine, and does not do them, will be like a foolish man who built his house on the sand: and the rain descended, the floods came, and the winds blew and beat on that house; and it fell. And great was its fall. (Matthew 7:24–27).

God wants His people to succeed in every area of life. When God said, "Let there be light," the earth was without shape or form, empty and void, and darkness was everywhere. When we read the Bible, the light of God comes into our lives, bringing order where there is confusion and light where there is darkness.

King David experienced many hardships, and he had many enemies. For years, he had to hide from King Saul. When the opportunity was presented to David to kill King Saul, David decided not to kill Saul but to wait on God for His divine justice:

> For You will light my lamp; the Lord my God will enlighten my darkness. (Psalm 18:28)

In times of darkness, confusion, indecision, and desperation, the Word of God can bring light and guidance. Do not be hasty to do things without consulting God and asking for guidance because failure can be at the door.

By reading God's Word, we can see that many people who came before us dealt with harsh things in their lives. The Bible is a tool to teach us what things will work for us and what things will not work for us. When we read the Bible, it reminds us that others before us grabbed this faith, held this faith, and remained in the confidence of God. Through their faith, they reached God. Through faith, many overcame obstacles and challenges:

> Subdued kingdoms, worked righteousness, obtained promises, stopped the mouth of lions, quenched violence of fire, escaped the edge of the sword, out of weakness were made strong, became valiant in battle, turned to flight the armies of the aliens. (Hebrews 11:33–34).

In reading the Bible, our faith grows and becomes stronger because the faith we preach today is the same one as the primitive church and the one that Abraham and his descendants cherished:

> Others were tortured, not accepting deliverance, that they might obtain a better resurrection. Still, others had trial of mockings and scourgings, yes, and of chain and imprisonment. They were stoned, they were sawn in two, were tempted, were slain with the sword. They wandered about in sheepskins and goat skins, being destitute, afflicted, tormented—of whom the world was not worthy. They wandered in deserts and mountains, in dens and caves of the earth. (Hebrews 11:35–38)

As Christians, it should not surprise us that we will experience persecutions, hardships, and afflictions. It happened in the past, it is happening right now, and it will continue until the return of our Jesus.

Reading and being doers of the Word helps Christians have the faith to stay strong against any adversity. Nonbelievers and

Christians will experience hardships, but we are better off with Christ. Christ helps us go through things and does not leave us alone. Paul knew that Timothy would experience hardships and encouraged him to be faithful to the end:

> But you be watchful in all things, endure affliction, do the work of an evangelist, fulfill your ministry. For I am already being poured out as a drink offering, and the time of my departure is at hand. I have fought the good fight, I have finished the race, I have kept the faith. Finally, there is laid up for the crown of righteousness, which the Lord, the righteous Judge, will give to me on that Day, and not to me only but also to all who have loved His appearing. (2 Timothy 4:5–8)

Paul did not sugarcoat his message; he presented it in love and truth. Paul was saying, "Timothy, you will experience afflictions, but hold on because this is part of our faith." Paul was telling him to focus on fulfilling the ministry. Paul seems to be saying, "I have kept the faith, and if I have done it, you can do it too." Being faithful against persecutions, afflictions, or challenges is part of how Christians testify the truth to the world and shine in the dark.

Once, I gave up on God and His promises concerning my life. I was, wholeheartedly, giving my all to help in ministry, but I soon realized that the enemy was at work even in the ministry. I could not bear the fact that leaders would turn against their own or accuse or lie against their own. Finally, God opened the door to leave this ministry, but I pretty much became discouraged about believing in ministry in my heart. I knew I had a calling, but I was burnt out. I was tired, sad, and depressed about all the things that went wrong in the ministry I had been a part of. Harming ministries is the expertise of the enemy. The enemy will bring confusion, disagreements, or divisions into ministries, and God's work will not continue. The enemy will use anybody—even leaders, pastors, evangelists, prophets, and other Christians—to damage or cause harm to brothers and sisters in Christ.

How can I shine while I am being persecuted by those I love or once loved? Betrayal is real, and it is the work of the devil. How can one stand in front of betrayal or rejection? Again, by standing on the Word of God. The Bible is full of great verses about trusting in the justice of God. God will avenge you from those who did you wrong or persecuted you. Declare and decree the Word of God:

- "Let all my enemies be ashamed and greatly troubled; let them turn back and be ashamed suddenly" (Psalm 6:10).
- "Behold, all those who were incensed against you shall be ashamed and disgraced; they shall be as nothing, and those who strive with you shall perish" (Isaiah 41:11).
- "But the Lord is with me as a mighty, awesome One. Therefore my persecutors will stumble, and will not prevail. They will be greatly ashamed, for they will not prosper. Their everlasting confusion will never be forgotten" (Jeremiah 20:11).
- "The Lord will cause your enemies who rise against you to be defeated before your face; they shall come out against you one way and flee before you seven ways" (Deuteronomy 28:7)

So many great verses speak of the power of God. He will fight for us, and He will bring divine justice against those that have afflicted us, persecuted us, or caused us harm. As Christians, we shine the most when we let God fight for us by standing on His Word. It is part of our faith. My brothers and sisters, we do not have to take vengeance into our own hands. We do not have to fight for ourselves. We do not have to avenge ourselves. Remember that our fight is not "against flesh and blood, but against principalities, against powers, against rulers of the darkness of this age, against spiritual hosts of wickedness in the heavenly places" (Ephesians 6:12).

I have learned that God is fighting for us Christians and protecting us. All our enemies are nothing. They are nowhere to be found. God has silenced their mouths. Today, God brought me back to my right place, and I am doing God's work today. I am fulfilling my ministry in Jesus's name. The works of the devil will never succeed, but the righteous ones who follow Jesus and do the will of God will surely succeed. The doers of the scriptures receive blessings. Amen.

CHAPTER TEN

DEFENDING
CHRISTIANITY

Beloved, let us love one another, for love is of God; and everyone who
loves is born of God and knows God. He who does not love does not
know God, for God is love. In this the love of God was manifested
toward us, that God has sent His only begotten Son into the world,
that we might live through him. In this is love, not that we loved God,
but that he loved us and sent His Son to be the propitiation for our
sins. Beloved, if God so loved us, we also ought to love one another.

—1 JOHN 4:7-11

Christianity is the only faith that proclaims that Jesus is alive. To
this day, many have proclaimed that they are the way. Muhammad
is dead. Buddha is dead. On the contrary, Christ Jesus has risen
from the dead and is alive. Jesus is the example of God's love
for humanity. God is love. Love is a choice. Everyone has the
power to choose to love. The opposite of love is *misos* in Greek,
which means "to hate or detest, especially to persecute." Most of
the authors of the books in the New Testament wrote in Greek.
The Greeks differentiated types of love, such as friendship love
(philos), family love (storge), romantic love (eros), but my focus

here is agape, which in the New Testament refers to the love of God. Agape represents the unconditional love of God toward humanity without any expectancy of receiving anything in return.

Today, the world uses the word *love* like it means nothing, and many people lack an understanding of what love is. For Christians, we know that God is love: "For God is love" (1 John 4:8). Since God is love, humans were created by love. The perfect example of the love of God is that He sent His only begotten Son to die for the sins of many:

> For God so loved the world that He gave His only begotten Son, that whoever believes in Him should not perish but have everlasting life. (John 3:16)

The elements of God's love are clear; He chose to create humans, He chose to love humanity, and He died for humanity to demonstrate His love. Now humanity has the power to choose to love God or to turn their backs on Him. Forcing this love on humanity is not how God works. Humanity has the free will to choose.

Jesus was fulfilling His ministry here on earth and setting the example of how to love:

> A new commandment I give to you, that you love one another; as I have loved you, that you also love one another. By this, all will know that you are My disciples if you have love for one another. (John 13:34–35)

Jesus demonstrated His compassion many times (Matthew 9:36). One way to defend Christianity is by showing compassion for those who persecute us. Unfortunately, Jesus had many enemies who persecuted Him.

Norman Geisler explained how we must model Jesus's unique character:

> Jesus's willing submission to the ignominious suffering and death by crucifixion, while maintained love and forgiveness toward those killing him, is proof of this virtue (Luke 23:34, 43).[29]

The Son of God left His throne to come to live among men as a poor man, and then He died as a criminal. Even though His death was painful, He did not utter words of revenge. He forgave His enemies because He knew they lacked understanding. Jesus was the perfect example of love, patience, kindness, and humility.[30]

To defend Christianity, we must love our neighbors. We must practice patience. We must practice compassion. We must practice humility. This is not easy, but Jesus commanded us to do so. If we are trying to escape the lake of fire, we must practice the beatitudes:

> Blessed are the poor in spirit,
> For theirs is the kingdom of heaven.
> Blessed are those who mourn,
> For they shall be comforted.
> Blessed are the meek,
> For they shall inherit the earth.
> Blessed are those who hunger and thirst for righteousness,
> For they shall be filled.
> Blessed are the merciful,

---

[29] Norman L. Geisler, *The Big Book of Christian Apologetics* (Grand Rapids: Baker Books, 2012), 86.
[30] Geisler, 86.

For they shall obtain mercy.
Blessed are the pure in heart,
For they shall see God.
Blessed are the peacemakers,
For they shall be called sons of God.
Blessed are those who are persecuted for
righteousness' sake,
For theirs is the kingdom of heaven.
Blessed are you when they revile and persecute you,
and say all kinds of evil against you falsely for
My sake.
Rejoice and be exceedingly glad, for great is your
reward in heaven,
for so they persecuted the prophets who were
before you. (Matthew 5:3–12)

Another way to defend Christianity is through love. How can we defend Christianity in a self-centered world? Paul wrote to Timothy about such behaviors:

But know this, that in the last days perilous times will come. For men will be lovers of themselves, lovers of money, boasters, proud, blasphemers, disobedient to parents, unthankful, unholy, unloving, unforgiving, slanderers, without self-control, brutal, despisers of good, traitors, headstrong, haughty, lovers of pleasure rather than lovers of God. (2 Timothy 3:1–4)

Paul explained that there will be perilous times, hard-to-bear times, troublesome times, and dangerous times. In the last days, many people will have an outward appearance of being lovers of God, but their hearts will be far from God. It means there will be a lack of love. Even more, the enemy will give many people a mindset of how love is supposed to look. Again, Christians know that God is love (1 John 4:8).

John explicitly gave an illustration of the love of God (1 John 4). If God is love, then Jesus is love, and if we have Jesus as our Savior, then we Christians, have the love of God.

Only God can break the lack of our willingness to love God. As Christians we preach Jesus. There are many ways to preach Jesus; but it is the work of the Holy Spirit to convict people of their sins. God has empowered the church with agape love. God has empowered the church with the fruit of the Holy Spirit. When we receive the Holy Spirit, we have the power to love and give testimony to God's love:

> If you then, being evil, know how to give good gifts to your children, how much more will your Father who is in heaven give good things to those who ask Him. (Matthew 7:11)

There is a difference between doing good works and being a Christian. Anybody can do good works or proclaim to be a good person. A follower of Jesus carries the pure agape love of God in his or her heart. Just because people do good works does not mean God is in their hearts. The love of God is real. When a person accepts Jesus, something magnificent happens in their heart.

How many people serve and follow other worldviews or worship idols made by human hands? How many professed to have love and professed to do good? Geisler said, "Only the supernatural love of God can motivate a person to express true agape."[31]

- "Greater love has no one than this, than to lay down one's life for his friends" (John 15:13).

---

[31] Geisler, 443.

- "For when we were still without strength, in due time Christ died for the ungodly. For scarcely for a righteous man will one die; yet perhaps for a good man someone would even dare to die. But God demonstrates His own love towards us, in that while we were still sinners, Christ died for us" (Romans 5:6–8).
- "Beloved, let us love one another, for love is of God; and everyone who loves is born of God and knows God" (1 John 4:7).

The sincere agape love is received by accepting Jesus and doing His will in our lives. This is not a gift from humans or angels but God. As long as atheists do not allow themselves to believe in God and accept Jesus, they will never experience true agape. On the other hand, when atheists acknowledge belief in the existence of God and repent from their sins, the love of God can come into their hearts.

Jesus gave instructions on how to love our enemies:

> You have heard that it was said, "You shall love your neighbor and hate your enemy." But I say to you, love your enemies, bless those who curse you, do good to those who hate you, and pray for those who spitefully use you and persecute you, that you may be sons of your Father in heaven; for He makes His sun rise on the evil and on the good, and send rain on the just and on the unjust. For if you love those who love you, what reward have you? Do not even the tax collectors do the same? And if you greet our brethren only, what do you do more than others? Do not even the tax collectors do so? Therefore you shall be perfect, just as your Father in heaven is perfect. (Matthew 5:43–48)

For Christians, many times, it is hard trying to be Christlike. It can be challenging, especially when one is hated, despised, or persecuted. But Jesus tells us to love our enemies, bless them, and pray for them. In the last chapter, I spoke about how God will avenge us against our enemies; just to clarify, I was referring to our fight against principalities, the power of darkness, the devil, or demons. Here, I am talking about humans. These can be neighbors, friends, family members, acquaintances, or coworkers. We can rebuke or bind the devil working through them and ask God to avenge us against those spiritual enemies. Jesus gave specific instructions saying that we are to love the people through which the enemy operates. We must bless them and pray for them. Remember that they are souls who may need salvation. As we stay grounded in walking in love toward our enemies, God will continue to do His work.

Paul acknowledges that the greatest gift Christians have received is the love of God. Therefore, Paul writes to the Corinthians and says that if one has faith to move mountains but does not have the love of God, one is nothing:

> Though I bestow all my goods to feed the poor, and though I give my body to be burned, but have not love, it profits me nothing. Love suffers long and is kind; love does not envy; love does not parade itself, is not puffed up; does not behave rudely, does not seek its own, is not provoked, thinks no evil; does not rejoice in iniquity, but rejoices in the truth; bears all things, believes all things, hopes all things, endures all things. (1 Corinthians 13:3–7)

You cannot give anyone something that you do not have. When Jesus died on the cross, He gave Himself. Jesus imparted to us the spirit of love. As Christians walk in the spirit of love, we experience similar things to Jesus, such as persecutions and victories. The spirit of love in us will attract those who do not have it. We will encounter evil people who are under the spirit of envy, rudeness, iniquity, persecution, adultery, fornication, uncleanliness, witchcraft, idolatry, and/or hatred. We will encounter others who lack love or are operating in the flesh or under the influence of evil spirits. As Christians, we need the gift of discerning of spirits to be in operation so we can distinguish what kind of spirits we are dealing with. With this gift in operation, God will give us wisdom and a strategy to demonstrate the love of God:

> For God has not given us a spirit of fear, but of power and of love of a sound mind. (2 Timothy 1:7)

God has given us the power of love. We have the spirit of love, and we have the power to love—so that others may know Jesus. Today, many religions and worldviews tell us humanity is still seeking something higher than themselves to fill an emptiness in our souls. Only God can fill this emptiness. God created humanity for the purpose of worshipping Him. Unfortunately, the manifestation of evil shows that the world lacks God and His love.

The demonstration of the love of God is Jesus. The only way to receive salvation is through Jesus Christ. Jesus said to Thomas, "I am the way, the truth, and the life. No one comes to the Father except through Me" (John 14:6). When preaching about Jesus to others, I have encountered many people who say that God is everywhere—and that God is Allah, Buddha, or any other god. Indeed, God is everywhere because the Word of God says, "The eyes of the Lord are in every place, keeping watch on the evil and the good" (Proverbs 15:3).

The devil speaks in half-truths and half-lies, but the true God that Christians serve is not the same God known to Muslims, Buddhists, or Hindus. This worldview that God is in all is known as *pantheism*. The idea that all people are serving the same God is false, and this lie comes from the devil. Other worldviews that fall into pantheism are New Age religions, Christian Science, Unity, and Scientology.[32] How can Christians demonstrate and distinguish that there is only one true God who gives true agape? By our fruit!

Many in the world are saying that each worldview is serving its own way to their true God. In reality, this statement is an error. The fruit of love confirms that Christians have the gift of love from God. He is Jesus. Jesus reminded His disciples that the only way a person can be saved and escape the flames of hell is through Him. The devil has fooled many people by making them believe they were serving the true God. If we want to prove that we serve the true God, we must be in alignment with God's Word and give birth to the fruit of love.

Bearing the fruit of love is a miracle. It is spiritual, and it is supernatural. Only God can help us receive the gift of love, receive the spirit of love, walk in the spirit of love, demonstrate the fruit of love, and give birth to the fruit of love. Since the gift of love is from God, Christians know that this is a miracle. In contrast, the worldview of pantheism accepts the following:

> Miracles are impossible. For if all is God, and God is all, nothing exists apart from God that could be interrupted or broken into, which is what the nature of a miracles requires.[33]

As Christians, we have within us the miracle of love. When we operate in love, we demonstrate the lack of understanding other worldviews have of the love of God. Jesus was an expert on miracles, and He instructed Christians to demonstrate the love of God in miracles. To work in the realm of miracles and

---

[32] Geisler, 425.
[33] Geisler, 426.

supernatural things, we must seek the presence of the Holy Spirit. In doing this, Christians will gain many souls walking on the wrong path of different worldviews that teach belief systems contrary to the truth.

Atheists bombard Christians with so many questions, but the notable one is this: If there is a loving God, then why does God allow people to suffer, die, or go to hell? The answer is simple. God is God, and He created the world for His glory. God set the rules from the beginning until the end. It is not the fault of God that the fall of man occurred. The fall of man confirms that God gave humanity free will. If God wanted it, He could have forced humanity to do His will. Geisler said, "Forced freedom is not freedom."[34] He added, "Since God is love, he cannot force himself on anyone against their will. Forced love is not love; it is rape."[35] The fact that atheists do not want to recognize there is a God shows the power of free will that God gave to humanity.

It is easier to accept that there is no Hell and live a life of temporal pleasure. God gives us true freedom, and we can only find true freedom in Him. Many people have lived their lives without accepting that God or Hell exists. When their time to depart from this world comes, entering an actual place called Hell will be disastrous. The lies and the devil's deceits are still real today—just as they were on the day of man's fall. Hell is an actual place, and it is a horrendous place that humans were never meant to be a part of.

Many people believe that Hell is here and now, but the reality is that Hell is a place, and it is not here, and it is not now. Jesus and the apostles preached about a place called hell. There are so many testimonies of people having experiences where God has taken them to Hell to testify so that others may come to know God and escape Hell. Since God does not and will not force

---

[34] Geisler, 144.
[35] Geisler, 144.

anyone to love Him or accept Him, Hell has been established to demonstrate God's sovereignty.

According to Geisler, Hell serves five purposes:

- "God's justice demands a hell because God is just (Romans 2).
- The love of God demands a hell because a God of love cannot force people to love Him.
- Human dignity demands a hell because God cannot force people into heaven against their free will.
- The sovereignty of God demands a hell because, without a hell, there no final victory over evil.
- The cross of Christ implies a hell, but why the cross and all this suffering unless there is a hell?"[36]

For atheists, it would be wiser to argue a standpoint that benefits their own salvation rather than to reason against God, His Word, and His establishments. Atheists do not believe they need salvation. Salvation was already being provided through Jesus Christ.

Once, I was sitting in the library, and a lady noticed I was reading a Christian apologetic book. She was intrigued, and we started a conversation. She stated that she used to be a Christian and had been raised in a Christian church, but now she was becoming a secular humanist. She said that she realized that science deserves more credit than God. Even though she had extraordinary experiences with God in the past, she was giving the glory and honor to science for saving her life and that of her son.

I said, "Who gives intelligence and knowledge to men?" It is God, my lovely readers! I told her that science confirms that there is a supernatural God who works in the supernatural realm to

---

[36] Geisler, 222.

demonstrate His power and glory. God revealed to Daniel that in the end-times, "knowledge shall increase" (Daniel 12:4). Science proves God and confirms God. Science is nothing without God. Humans are nothing without God. God gives pleasure to humans to gain knowledge so that science can advance, but the devil has distorted the thoughts of humans. They are turning their backs on the Creator, turning to themselves, and glorifying man-made ideas and things.

The lady quickly changed the subject to historical facts, adding that the church impeded science from progressing by not allowing humans to open bodies so science could improve. I agreed with her. This is a historical fact, but only to the Catholic Church, which impeded science's advancement and condemned science. Maybe their reason was to continue to have control over the people or because they feared the unknown. However, that does not give us the right to deny God or reject Christians today. I encouraged her not to get stuck in historical facts and to revive herself in experiencing Jesus as alive and doing great things among those who seek Him. It is good to know the history, but Jesus is not dead. He is alive, and He is still revealing Himself to people.

Many Christians are turning their backs on the cross of Jesus and are crediting science for their healing or interventions. Some Christians are becoming atheists for the love of science and the advancement of science. Christians, let us not lose focus on who God is in our lives. Christians, let us not lose focus on what Jesus did on the cross for the remission of our sin. I call on Christians around the world to continue carrying the cross and fulfilling our call or ministry. Let us continue to press on so we may receive the rewards of God and escape the flames of Hell.

CONCLUSION

Christians, we are living in critical times, and more than ever, we need to be firm in Christ Jesus. I hope this book inspires Christians worldwide to not lose track of who they are in Christ, pursue with fire God's will for their lives, and fulfill their ministries. God fulfilled His promises concerning His Son.

The life of Jesus proved to the world that God keeps His promises, and His words cannot be voided. Jesus led by example and fulfilled His ministry, giving us an example to follow. Let us remember that God used the prophets to announce the coming of the Messiah. Then, we see how He told His disciples to wait for the promise, and as we know, this came to pass.

The Son of Man told His disciples that a Second Coming would occur. The apostles consented and assured us that the Second Coming of Christ was inevitable in their writings. The church that God will raise will be ready, but in my heart, I know that the current church is not prepared.

Many Christians around the world are dealing with spiritual tiredness or fatigue, and many are sleeping. Many Christians have lost their first love—their fire for Jesus—and are consumed with worries about the world. God has given the church power, and I pray that the church will use this power. I pray that nothing will hold Christians back from experiencing the power of God in their lives and demonstrating to others the power of God so others may know God.

The primitive church took advantage of the scripture, took advantage of the power, and fulfilled its ministry, birthing Christianity even through persecution. I pray that today's church will take advantage of the scriptures and stand firm on the Word. I pray that the church will take advantage of the power of Christ Jesus, fulfill the ministry, and preach the gospel around the world.

Christians have power through Jesus, and His resurrection still testifies that He is alive and ready to help Christians around the world conquer their fears and advance in the kingdom. Christians acknowledge that the existence of evil is real, and it is in the atmosphere, but true Christians should stand against it. I pray that Christians will give good testimony and not be evildoers so that the gospel will advance. I pray that Christians around the world will awaken, rise, shine, and defend Christ!

BIBLIOGRAPHY

Berković, Daniel. "Beware of dogs! The position and role of dogs in biblical discourse." *KAIROS - Evangelical Journal of Theology*, 2014: 75-84.

Biblestudy.org. n.d. https://www.biblestudy.org/bibleref/meaning-of-numbers-in-bible/3.html (accessed 2020).

Brand, Charles, Charles Draper, and Archie England. *Holman Illustrated Bible Dictionary.* Nashville: Holman Bible Publishers, 2003.

Brown, Michael L. *Can You Be Gay and Christian?* Lake Mary: Charisma House Book Group, 2014.

Carson, D. A., and Douglas J. Moo. *Introduction to the New Testament.* Grand Rapids: Zondervan, 2009.

Cooper, Rodney L., and Max Anders. *Holman New Testament Commenetary Mark.* Nashville: Broadman & Holman Publishers, 2000.

Dictionary.com. n.d. http://www.dictionary.com/browse/openness?s=ts.

Edgar, William, and K. Scott Oliphint. *Christian Apologetics: Past and Present.* Wheaton: Crossway Books, 2009.

Estes, Daniel J. *Handbook on the Wisdom Books and Psalms.* Grand Rapids: BakerAcademic, 2005.

Foxe, John. *Foxe's Book of Martyrs.* London: John Day, 1563.

Geisler, Norman L.. *The Big Book of Christian Apologetics.* Grand Rapids: BakerBooks, 2012.

Gray, Rebecca. *Prophetic Figures in Late Second Temple Jewish Palestine: The Evidence of Josephus.* New York: Oxford University Press, 1993.

Habermas, Gary R., and Michael R. Licona . *The Case for the Resurrection of Jesus.* Grand Rapids: Kregel Publications, 2004.

Josephus, Flavius. *Antiquities of the Jews.* Rome, 75 AD.

Kaatz, Kevin W. *Early Controversies and the Growth of Christianity.* Santa Barbara: Praeger, 2012.

Kidner, Derek. *Genesis: An Introduction and Commentary.* Downers Grove: IVP Academic, 1967.

Lake, John G. *Spiritual Hunger The God-Men.* Dallas: Christ for the Nations, Inc., 1982.

Licona, Michael R. *The Resurrection of Jesus: A New Historical Approach.* Downers Grove: InterVarsity Press, 2010.

Martin, Walter. *The Kingdom of the Cults.* Bloomington: Bethany House, 2019.

Ortiz, Luis M. *Biblical Instructions for the Newly Converted (Instrucciones Biblicas para los Recien Convertidos.* Santafe de Bogota: Ediciones Antropos LTDA, 1994.

Radmacher, Earl, Ron Allen, and H. Wayne House. *Compact Bible Commentary*. Nashville: Thomas Nelson, 2004.

Stern, David H. *The Complete Jewish Study Bible*. Peabody: Hendrickson Publishers Marketing, LLC, 2016.

Strong, James. *Strong's Greek Hebrew Dictionary*. 1890.

Weaver, C. Douglas, and Rady Roldan-Figueroa. *Exploring Christian Heritage*. Waco: Baylor University Press, 2017.

Weber, Stuart K., and Max Anders. *Holman New Testament: Matthew*. Nashville: Broadman & Holman Publishers, 2000.

Printed in the United States
by Baker & Taylor Publisher Services